ISBN 0-942604-26-1
Library of Congress Catalog
Card Number 92-060969

**Distributed to the trade in the United States
and Canada by :**
Van Nostrand Reinhold
115 Fifth Avenue
New York, NY 10003

**Distributed throughout the rest of the
world by:**
Hearst Books International
1350 Avenue of the Americas
New York, NY 10019

Published by:
Madison Square Press
10 East 23rd Street
New York, NY 10010

**International Logos & Trademarks Design
Competition is a Project of:**
Supon Design Group, Inc.
1000 Connecticut Avenue, NW, Suite 415
Washington, DC 20036

Printed in Hong Kong

INTERNATIONAL LOGOS & TRADEMARKS II

ACKNOWLEDGMENTS

International Logos & Trademarks II

Project Director
Supon Phornirunlit

Communications Director
Wayne Kurie

Judges
Stuart Ash
Douglas Doolittle
Jay Vigon
Marilyn Worseldine

Art Director
Supon Phornirunlit

Concept Designer
Rex Peteet, Sibley/Peteet

Managing Editor
Wayne Kurie

Production Coordinator
Andrew Berman

Photographer
Barry Myers

Writer
Linda Klinger

Supon Design Group
International Book Division Staff
Dianne Cook
Andrew Dolan
Richard Lee Heffner
Brett Nation
Dave Prescott

Volunteers
Lisa Brzezniak
Michael Chinn
Jennifer Lowe
Bruce Morgan
Hien Nguyen
Patrick O'Brien
Dave Zambotti

Technical Support
Susan Rubel

Desktop Publishing
microPRINT, Washington, D.C.

A very special thank you to:
Kelli F. Bartlett
Kelly Crossley
Frank Parsons Paper Company, Inc.
Gerald McConnell
Peggy Stoltzfus
Scott Stoltzfus

CONTENTS

COMMENTARY

Supon Phornirunlit

It takes a skilled designer to discover and unleash the emotional content of a logo. The designer's ability to control the symbol successfully will also serve to call up attitudes about it from its audience: strength, professionalism, playfulness or elegance. As in previous years, our judges — representing decades of experience creating internationally acclaimed graphics — were well-qualified to find great designs in stacks of possibilities. Working with judges Jay, Marilyn, Douglas and Stuart offered us yet another opportunity to learn about the direction of trademark design in the 1990s, while we honored those who have worked hard to restore personality and life to an art that is so difficult to do well.

Whittling thousands of trademark entries down to the very best compositions of form, line and message is a time-consuming task. The Supon Design Group staff and our diligent quartet contemplated row after row of neatly arranged logos, stationery, posters and packaging to come up with this representative sample of some of the best in the business. The quality of this year's entries was exceptionally high, and our judges spent a great deal of time in discussion and thought.

Every design competition has some quirks, as did this one. For example, judges are usually confronted with several elements that, for some reason, appear often enough

that they seem to herald the latest fad. In 1992, it was lightbulbs, eagles and airbrush techniques. Familiar icons, such as horses, were used frequently. Artists had to come up with new ways to draw the icon for it to work. A few succeeded, in startling and delightful ways.

"Violate a cliché, and it becomes powerful," explained Marilyn. "Have an icon do what it's never done before, or what you never expected, and it's almost certainly award-winning."

The trademarks presented an interesting look at the way businesses around the world were portrayed, and offered glimpses into the

values of each society. This year, more entries tended to be artistic or whimsical than cool and abstract. The marks made a statement about the struggling economy worldwide, with fewer expensive corporate packages entered than in past years and less embossing. There seemed to be an emphasis on environmental sensitivity, with designers using more environmentally friendly paper and less gloss, bleeds and foil-stamping. "The pendulum has swung back to the economical quality of design, emphasizing the craft," said Stuart, citing the movement towards more subtle and sensitive use of materials.

Our group of judges applauded originality when they found it, and they found it in unusual places. They enjoyed discovering a lack of control ("designers are often too controlled"), a return to the basics ("I like the simplicity when they just do it right"), and an emphasis on market orientation ("this would make me buy their product"). Logos failed because a judge would not want to look at it every day, or because too much time was spent trying to understand what it was or what it was trying to say.

The job of a juror panel is much more difficult than it seems. They must consider all the idiosyncracies of a competition when making their choices, and strive to make the fairest calls. For example, it would have been much easier to review work on one level — its immediate impression. The public,

COMMENTARY

however, sees the work in the context of the marketplace, and usually in its full application. Our judges had to keep this in mind for a fair assessment.

But despite their drawbacks, competitions remain one of the best ways a designer can measure his or her work. Marilyn's inspiration may not benefit from winning an award, but awards help her discover where she is in relation to her peers. "Competitions operate as a summation of your work at the moment," she said. "If you're included in a show, you know you're probably doing good work." Jay shunned most contests until he realized they were a major source of public relations promotion for his work. Now he enters several annually. Douglas also stayed away until recently, because he feared his ideas may be stolen. Involvement in competitions prompted him to reassess the value of awards.

"The quality of your work doesn't change with a competition," he said. "You can sit on your work for years, then there's suddenly a limelight and you're directed under it."

"But," insisted Jay, "the only way to improve your work is to keep working. Not by entering more contests."

The trademarks presented an interesting look at the way businesses around the world were portrayed, and offered glimpses into the values of each society.

So when it was all over, we asked ourselves what we had learned about the components of a good logo. As usual, we came up with several answers. A logo may only be one part of a system of corporate identity, but it is often the most important because it is the essence of the company personality. It is the attitude of what it represents. How well or poorly the logo carries this off reflects directly on that company. The skill of the designer is critical to give the company's personality form. When it came time to choose, design that had been done with integrity, heart and soul quickly rose to the top. The pieces found in this book each demonstrate an intensity of feeling and innovative thought, and communicate corporate personality in memorable and positive ways.

Summarized Douglas: "There are no such thing as rivals in this industry. If they are better than me, I learn; if I am better than them, they learn. There are only winners." I'd like to thank those designers who helped reinforce this concept through their work, and we extend our congratulations to the designers of a few of the best marks in the world.

Supon Phornirunlit is owner of Supon Design Group, Inc., where he serves as creative director, and art director. He founded the company in 1988, and since, he and his design team have earned over 240 awards, including recognition from every major national design competition. His studio's work has appeared in publications such as Graphis, Communication Arts, Print, Studio *and* How. *Currently, Supon is on the board of directors of the Art Directors' Club of Metropolitan Washington and is project director of the International Logos & Trademarks awards competition. Supon and SDG have been featured in* How *magazine and the American Institute of Graphic Arts' (AIGA)* Journal, *as well as in the Asian magazine* Media Delite. *He has appeared on cable television's "Alexandria Journal" program, and was a guest on Asian radio. He regularly speaks at various organizations and schools.*

BEHIND THE SCENES

Wayne Kurie

Three hundred and nine winning pieces from 122 studios and 19 countries. Twelve pieces considered outstanding, meriting an additional award of excellence.

In a nutshell, those are the results of the second biannual competition of International Logos & Trademarks. I invite you to examine, contemplate, scrutinize — and learn from — these winning works of art, all of which are pictured herein. Indeed, that is the purpose of this book. But how did we get here from there? What happened behind the scenes? During judging? Before, and after? It was a lively journey that began one summer day in 1990, the day after the judging of our first competition.

We began by commissioning one of the judges from our last competition, Rex Peteet of Sibley/Peteet in Dallas, to design the event's identity. After ably creating the logo and call for entries, Peteet then translated the art into a colorful T-shirt, worn by most of us during judging.

We sent the call for entries poster to thousands of studios worldwide — to all previous entrants and to designers on selected international mailing lists. Based on prior experience, we knew that no matter how far in advance we mailed the invitations, most entries wouldn't arrive much before the deadline. And despite our mailing reminder postcards and extending the deadline more than once, we were right: Two-thirds of the three thousand entries arrived in our studio in the last few days before judging.

The judges were also arriving. We had invited each of the four jurors to a welcoming dinner the evening before judging was to begin. Thus, Stuart Ash and his girlfriend flew in from Toronto, Canada; Douglas Doolittle of Tokyo, from business in Hawaii, and Jay Vigon, his wife, and two daughters (who turned the trip to the nation's capital into a week-long vacation), from Los Angeles. Judge Marilyn Worseldine had the easiest commute: She walked the few blocks from her Georgetown home to the Sheraton City Centre, the site of the weekend-long judging. As this roster of design professionals made clear, our most important objective in the selection of judges was diversity — diversity in style and type of work, size and specialty of design firm, geographical origin, and breadth of work. We feel we succeeded quite well.

Although their actual criteria was unwritten and unspoken, all four judges were in agreement as to what they were looking for. First, they said, was concept — probably the single most important element on which the work was judged. Then came assessments of appropriateness, memorableness, distinctiveness, reproducibility, visualization, execution, and impact: A good logo must, of course, be appropriate. It must be capable of being reproduced in different media — the flap of an envelope, the back of a T-shirt or the side of a truck, for instance. Execution is critical. We've all seen great ideas become impotent when poorly rendered. Visually, logos must be articulated well. Lines must be drawn straight when meant to be, or perfectly symmetrical, if that's the objective. Impact is something that touches the viewer and makes an impression beyond the superficial. Vigon told of a moving company in Japan whose logo is a mother cat carrying her kitten, which distills a world of emotions — including care, responsibility, and gentleness — into a single image.

The actual judging filled an entire two days of an unseasonably cool (and sometimes rainy) weekend in August. Approximately three thousand entries were received, then divided into the following six categories: Company Logos, Product or Event Logos, Stationery, Packaging, Other Applications, and Campaigns. Preliminary judging was to occur on Saturday, with final selections made on Sunday. The judges felt that this two-part process was helpful in

Continued on page xi

Supon Design Group staff and volunteers (clockwise from upper left): *Andrew Dolan, Richard Lee Heffner, Dave Zambotti, Dave Prescott, Mike Chinn, Patrick O'Brien, Wayne Kurie, Lisa Brzezniak, Hien Nguyen;* (not pictured: *Dianne Cook, Jennifer Lowe, Bruce Morgan*)

BEHIND THE SCENES

evaluating the work. "On the first day, we just looked at the symbols," said Ash. "But after revisiting them the next day, we all benefited from a fresh eye."

Saturday proceeded as planned. The four judges sat at a table across from two members of Supon Design Group's staff. In turn, the staffpersons picked up each piece and individually showed them to the judges. The judges were directed to evaluate each piece on its own merit. Each judge indicated his or her preference as to whether or not the piece should win by holding up either a "Yes" or "No" sign. Any piece receiving at least one yes was in contention and up for final consideration on Sunday. Those not receiving any yes's were discarded. Posters, packaging, and other large or unweildy pieces were displayed on a table in another room. All were tagged with an identification number corresponding to those on scorecards given the judges. The members of the jury then gave either a "Yes" or "No" to each piece by marking the appropriate box on his or her sheet. Votes were tabulated following the methodology above.

To avoid conflicts of interest, we made it clear to the judges that they would have to award a "No" vote to any piece designed by him or herself or by anyone from his or her studio. (This, of course, did not mean that these pieces would not win, however, as

pieces with one, two, three, or four yes's could win.) Also, to better evaluate the entries, judges were permitted to ask for the name of the client, nature of the client's business, or country in which the piece was designed. Judges were not permitted to know the name of the designer or design firm that created the piece.

Saturday ended with 672 pieces receiving at least one "Yes." The next morning, these were all spread out on tables for the judges to finalize their selections. Up to this point, all judging had been an individual matter. This would be different on Sunday. For a piece to make the final cut, the judges' decisions had to be unanimous. As a team, the four judges walked around the room, discussing the merits and/or demerits of each and every piece. This fostered much discussion, yielding agreements and disagreements. All of this was very telling: Four diverse designers, from different backgrounds, talented in different styles, and experienced in different ways, all discussing others' work. It did make for an interesting Sunday morning. By midday, the judges had made their final selections: Three hundred and nine pieces would be featured in the book.

But the judges were not yet finished. New to the process this year, we asked them to make one more decision. From all the winning pieces, the judges were instructed to

select several (the exact number was wholly up to them) meriting additional praise. We titled this distinction the Award of Outstanding Achievement. The only limitation we gave the judges was to tell them that, for this award, pieces from their own studios or Supon Design Group would not be eligible. Working together, the judges selected twelve of the 309 winning pieces to receive this special award. Its recipients were varied, comprising seven studios, from four countries, and four categories. These pieces are featured in a special section at the beginning of this book.

In my role as the competition's communications director, I would like to thank all who participated. This includes the entire Supon Design Group staff and volunteers, all of whom were exemplary; the judges, who worked tirelessly for several days straight, for giving of themselves and of their professions; and especially, to the thousands of designers who submitted work, thus building the foundation for this event. I thank you all.

Wayne Kurie is marketing manager at Supon Design Group, Inc. He earned a Bachelor of Arts degree in marketing management from the University of Hartford and then went on to complete his MBA in international business at The George Washington University in Washington, D.C. He is communications director of Supon Design Group's International Book Division, in which capacity he also serves as managing editor. His talents have been recognized by several regional and national awards competitions.

JUDGES

> "Have an icon do what it's never done before, or what you never expected, and it's almost certainly award-winning."
>
> Marilyn Worseldine

Stuart Ash
Gottschalk + Ash International
Toronto, Ontario, Canada

Stuart Ash is a founder and principal of Gottschalk + Ash International, a design and consulting firm with offices in Montréal, Toronto, Zurich, and Milan. His work has been exhibited in the Mead Library of Ideas in New York, the National Gallery of Canada, and the Montréal Museum of Fine Arts as well as many specialized exhibitions throughout the world. He has been published in most major design magazines in Japan, the United States, and Europe.

Ash received the Canadian Centennial Medal for his creation of the Canadian centennial symbol. He has also developed a comprehensive wayfinding program and identity for Path, Toronto's underground pedestrian walkway. He is a member of the Society of Graphic Designers of Canada, the American Institute of Graphic Arts, the Alliance Graphique Internationale, and the Royal Canadian Academy of the Arts.

Douglas Doolittle
Douglas Design Office
Tokyo, Japan

Douglas Doolittle is art director and principal of Douglas Design Office in Tokyo, which he established in 1979. He has assisted several major Japanese companies with their corporate and brand identities, as well as with related projects developing catalogues, posters, packaging, and other products. His clientele also includes corporations in Canada, Hong Kong, the Netherlands, Taiwan, and the United States.

Doolittle has been honored with the Gold Award for International Poster Competition in the United States, as well as numerous other design awards in Canada, Japan, and the United States. His design work has appeared in over 40 publications in six countries, and in 1991 he lectured at the International Council of Graphic Design Associations in Montréal, on the theme "Convergence of Business and Design."

JUDGES

Jay Vigon
Jay Vigon Design & Art Direction
Los Angeles, California, USA

In 1986, Jay Vigon published his first book, *Marks*, a retrospective of his inventive logo design. The response was unprecedented and established the Los Angeles-based designer as one of the most resourceful and versatile innovators in the field. A graduate of Art Center College of Design in southern California, he earned a reputation during the 1970s designing classic logos for some of America's best-known record albums and movie campaigns. In the 1980s, he was a partner in Vigon Seireeni, one of Los Angeles's premier design and advertising firms, where he created images for major companies in the entertainment and fashion industries.

Today, Vigon continues his conceptual approach to creative problem-solving on his own. He works from the studio of his Laurel Canyon, California, home, which he shares with his wife, illustrator Margo Nahas, and his two young daughters.

Marilyn Worseldine
Market Sights, Inc.
Washington, D.C., USA

Marilyn Worseldine is vice president of Market Sights, Inc., in Washington, D.C. Her design work has appeared in *Print*, *Communication Arts*, *Trademarks and Symbols of the World*, *International Logos and Trademarks*, and *Letterheads*. She has won Gold, Silver, and Distinctive Merit awards from the Art Directors Club of Metropolitan Washington and Silver from the New York Art Directors Club. She also has been included in both the local and national shows of AIGA.

Prior to forming Market Sights in 1975, Worseldine was creative director of Frank James Productions in St. Louis. While working in St. Louis, she received various awards from the St. Louis Art Directors Club, including Best of Show, Gold, Silver, and Distinctive Merit awards. She studied at the Kansas City Art Institute and received a degree in fine arts from Webster University.

> "There are no such things as rivals in this industry. If they are better than me, I learn; if I am better than them, they learn. There are only winners."
>
> Douglas Doolittle

OUTSTANDING ACHIEVEMENT AWARDS

DU VERRE GLASS

Design Firm: Concrete Design Communications Inc., Toronto, Ontario, Canada
Art Directors: John Pylypczak, Diti Katona
Designer: Diti Katona
Photographer: Chris Nicholls

Logo
Du Verre Glass is a Toronto retailer of fine tableware, glassware and housewares. Their mark combines pictures and type to leave an impression "with a richness to it," agreed our judges. They found the quality of the solution excellent and easily reproducible in a multitude of sizes. Lines are softened by screens and circles, creating a dream-like figure with a great deal of finesse. And, typographically, our judges called this trademark unique and outstanding.

ENDURA NAIL COMPANY

Design Firm: RBMM, Dallas, Texas, USA
Art Director & Designer: Mat Alancheril

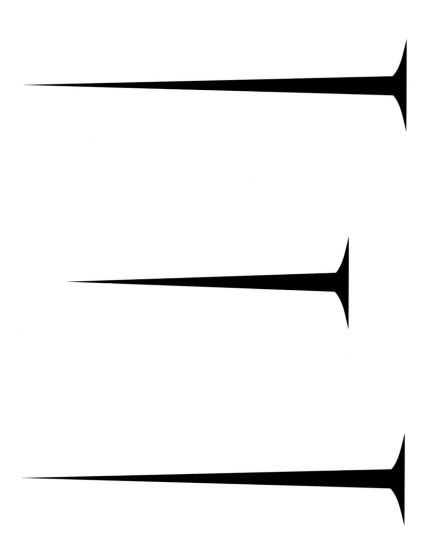

Logo
"Compact, brief and effective," describes this artwork for a nail
manufacturer. One judge summarized its attributes thusly:
"It is the perfect idea coming to a great execution, and looking effortless."
The marriage between a company name and its product — difficult to
achieve — worked particularly well here. The trademark also embodies
natural movement in an image both delicate and sharp, simultaneously.

FACIAL AESTHETIC SYSTEMS

Design Firm: RBMM, Dallas, Texas, USA
Art Director & Designer: Luis D. Acevedo

Logo

"A whimsical design," one judge rightly called it. Facial Aesthetic Systems' mark was designed to work for a company that creates personal cosmetic palettes for professional make-up artists and the general public. The judges applauded the artistic use of the mask/face with the attractive look of a Geisha girl. Its fascinating and memorable stylization leaves one with the ultimate impression of beauty. But there's also a bit of humor here — something fun is going on just out of sight, behind the scenes.

NOVA CINEMAS PTY. LTD.

Design Firm: Brian Sadgrove & Associates, Alberta Park, Victoria, Australia
Art Director & Designer: Brian Sadgrove

C I N E M A

NOVA

Logo

Cinema Nova is an Australian twin cinema arthouse. The logo successfully
complements both the theater and its genre of films, while enhancing
and becoming part of the cinema's interior design. The cinema's
architecture is startlingly eclectic, a good match for these graphics.
The judges found the typography a challenge that was perfectly resolved.
They acknowledged the logo's "Hollywood, almost special-effects feel,"
which embodied a certain nostalgia in a solution very well executed.

SEIBU

Design Firm: Alan Chan Design Company, Hong Kong, Hong Kong
Art Director: Alan Chan
Designers: Alan Chan, Phillip Leung
Illustrator: Gary Cheung

Logo
When Seibu — one of the Orient's largest department store chains —
opened its Hong Kong division, it wanted to convey a novel image to
its new customer base. This powerful logo uses ancient Chinese motifs
for inspiration. Two intertwining carp speak to the cultural belief that
even numbers are lucky, and simultaneously form the initial "S" of Seibu.
A study of Chinese culture also reveals that the word for "fish" is closely
related to the word for "abundance," further deepening the meaning
of this intriguing artwork.

DU VERRE GLASS

Design Firm: Concrete Design Communications Inc., Toronto, Ontario, Canada
Art Directors: John Pylypczak, Diti Katona
Designer: Diti Katona
Photographer: Chris Nicholls

Stationery

The Du Verre Glass letterhead exemplifies the upscale grace and delicacy
of this retailer's line of specialty wares. Its letterhead not only clearly
communicates the product line, but accurately captures the classic tone,
impressing our judges with its unusual face, which they found elegant.
But the design also had a quality "beyond beautiful," said one judge.
Said another, "The grays and black and white values work incredibly well.
It's not just a rubber-stamp solution."

ITALIA

Design Firm: Hornall Anderson Design Works, Seattle, Washington, USA
Art Director: Jack Anderson
Designers: Jack Anderson, Julia LaPine

Stationery

Italia is many things — a restaurant, deli and bakery that also offers
customers catering services, a wine shop and an art gallery. This diverse
organization deserved a thoughtful letterhead. "All of its stylizations
are complementary," said one judge. "It serves the products well."
The viewer's eye is drawn first to the cheerful, festive symbols. In this
application, the design also casts Italia as a professional firm, but with an
interest in providing a fun, joyful atmosphere for its clientele.

PACIFIC GUEST SUITES

Design Firm: Hornall Anderson Design Works, Seattle, Washington, USA
Art Director & Designer: Julia LaPine

Stationery

Our judges recognized Pacific Guest Suites, an organization providing
extended-stay accommodations, for its outstanding and congenial
letterhead. They found the careful use of copper and black colors tasteful,
and proposed that both the color choice and the clever idea elevated the
trademark to an even higher level. "The natural inclination would have
been to 'punch' a standard flower feel, but this designer resisted it."
The result was a logo without hard edges — a warm, humanistic symbol
that says "welcome."

COY, LOS ANGELES

Design Firm: COY, Los Angeles, California, USA
Art Director & Designer: John Coy

Single Application

This translucent business card for the California design firm COY was
a natural for an award in the Single Application category. An inventive
attempt, it succeeded because of its sensitivity to light, color and type.
Said one judge, "It's a gem of typography. It's like a lovely art project."
The card incorporates many disciplines of excellent design, such
as proportion and size, and its use of ink on both sides make it truly
unique by creating a new combination of overlapping images that
could be constructed no other way.

Z PREPRESS

Design Firm: Arias Associates, Palo Alto, California, USA
Art Director: Mauricio Arias
Designers: Ellen Bruni, Catherine Richards

Single Application

This recyclable envelope with a dog motif is one of a series of envelopes
that transport work between design and prepress firms. The judges
awarded the compelling artwork an achievement in the Application
category, noting that it was not an abstract corporate symbol, but told an
intriguing story. They identified the speed of turnover factor in the image
of the dog (a greyhound, they surmised), and liked the animal's artistic
interpretation. "It looks like it was dropped out of an aboriginal village,"
said one. "This logo should encourage designers to look at
overused images from a different perspective."

ITALIA

Design Firm: Hornall Anderson Design Works, Seattle, Washington, USA
Art Director: Jack Anderson
Designers: Jack Anderson, Julia LaPine

Campaign

Italia's campaign takes the same carefree symbols used in its letterhead,
warms them up, and scatters them over a variety of objects, prompting
an inviting and pleasant sensation in the viewer. Our quartet of judges
praised this campaign that worked well from labelling to T-shirts,
calling it wonderful and friendly. The loose drawing style and light
colors, they said, made Italia appear to be a place one would want to visit
often — fresh and informal. "The colors are so buttery and warm,
you may be tempted to eat this series of designs."

SEIBU

Design Firm: Alan Chan Design Company, Hong Kong, Hong Kong
Art Director: Alan Chan
Designers: Alan Chan, Phillip Leung
Illustrator: Gary Cheung

Campaign

The Seibu trademark flows through the campaign, symbolizing the
non-stop energy of both the fish image and the people who support this
upscale business concern. This energy seems to go to the center
of the logo, provoked by the simulated actions of the carp. Their large eyes
and the heavy gold color evoke additional impressions of strength. As this
pair of creatures work together to form a fascinating study of cultural icons
and commercial art, they also smooth away the occasional friction between
the Japanese and Hong Kong lifestyles, forming a seamless unity.

MERIT AWARDS

Client:
Advanced Surgical/Noonan Russo
Nature of Business:
Surgical instruments
Design Firm:
Pentagram Design
Art Director:
Woody Pirtle
Designer:
Woody Pirtle, John Klotnia

Client:
Agincourt Badminton Club
Nature of Business:
Badminton club
Design Firm:
Graphic Design Systems
Art Director:
Garry Lay
Designer:
Garry Lay

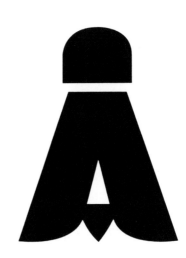

Client:
Atomic Ironworks
Nature of Business:
Ironwork
Design Firm:
Pentagram Design
Art Director:
Susan Hochbaum
Designer:
Susan Hochbaum

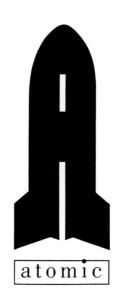

atomic

ADVANCED
SURGICAL

ADVANCED
SURGICAL

ADVANCED SURGICAL INC
305 COLLEGE ROAD EAST PRINCETON NJ 08540 / T 609 987 2340 / F 609 987 2342

Client:
Advanced Surgical/Noonan Russo
Nature of Business:
Surgical Instruments
Design Firm:
Pentagram Design
Art Director:
Woody Pirtle
Designer:
Woody Pirtle, John Klotnia

Client:
Atheneum Hotel
Nature of Business:
Hospitality
Design Firm:
Pentagram Design
Art Director:
Colin Forbes, Michael Gericke
Designer:
Michael Gericke
Illustrator:
Mirko Ilic

Client:
Tony Armour Photography
Nature of Business:
Photography
Design Firm:
VSA Partners, Inc.
Art Director:
Chris Froeter
Designer:
Chris Froeter

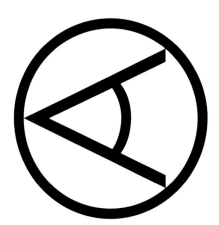

Client:
Corgan Associates
Nature of Business:
Architecture
Design Firm:
Pentagram Design
Art Director:
Woody Pirtle
Designer:
Woody Pirtle

Client:
Capp Street Project
Nature of Business:
Experimental art venue
Design Firm:
Morla Design, Inc.
Art Director:
Jennifer Morla
Designer:
Jennifer Morla, Sharrie Brooks

Capp Street Project

270 14th Street

San Francisco, CA 94103

Capp Street Project

270 14th Street

San Francisco

CA 94103

415.626.7747

Fax 415.626.7991

Capp Street Project

270 14th Street

San Francisco

CA 94103

415.626.7747

Fax 415.626.7991

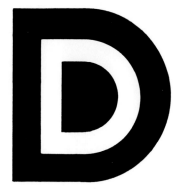

Client:
Dangle Design
Nature of Business:
Design
Design Firm:
Dangle Design
Art Director:
Mark Dangle
Designer:
Mark Dangle

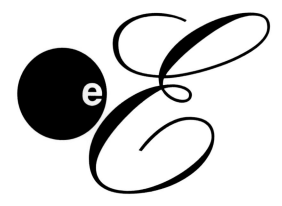

Client:
Werkbund
Nature of Business:
Multimedia publications and presentations
Design Firm:
Werkbund
Art Director:
Gregory Roll
Designer:
Gregory Roll
Typesetter:
A to A Graphics

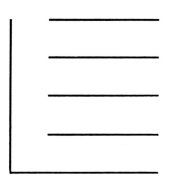

Client:
Levin School of Music
Nature of Business:
Music instruction
Design Firm:
Pat Taylor Inc.
Art Director:
Pat Taylor
Designer:
Pat Taylor

Client:
Everly Elevator Co.
Nature of Business:
Repair work
Design Firm:
Pat Taylor Inc.
Art Director:
Pat Taylor
Designer:
Pat Taylor

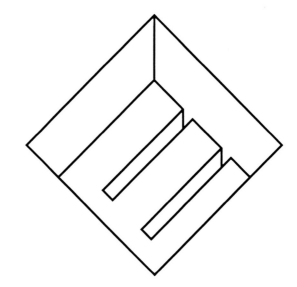

Client:
Visual Edge
Nature of Business:
Digital imaging
Design Firm:
Bright & Associates
Art Director:
Keith Bright
Designer:
Mark Verlander

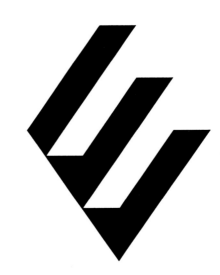

Client:
Fine Line Features
Nature of Business:
Film production
Design Firm:
Pentagram Design
Art Director:
Woody Pirtle
Designer:
Woody Pirtle

VISUAL EDGE

VISUAL EDGE

750R GATEWAY BOULEVARD SOUTH SAN FRANCISCO CA 94080 FAX 415 873 5958 TEL 415 873 5090

750R GATEWAY BOULEVARD SOUTH SAN FRANCISCO CA 94080 FAX 415 873 5958 TEL 415 873 5090

Client:
Visual Edge
Nature of Business:
Digital imaging
Design Firm:

Client:
Gotham Equities
Nature of Business:
Investment
Design Firm:
Pentagram Design
Art Director:
Michael Bierut
Designer:
Michael Bierut, Dorit Lev

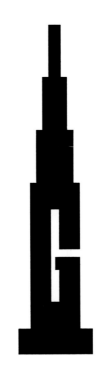

Client:
Gail Look-Yan Design
Nature of Business:
Graphic design and illustration
Design Firm:
Gail Look-Yan Design
Art Director:
Gail Look-Yan
Designer:
Gail Look-Yan

Client:
Goucher College
Nature of Business:
College
Design Firm:
F.E. Worthington, Inc.

HIRASUNA EDITORIAL

HIRASUNA EDITORIAL

DELPHINE HIRASUNA

901 BATTERY STREET
SUITE 212
SAN FRANCISCO, CA 94111
TEL. 415.986.8014
FAX. 415.986.7649

HIRASUNA EDITORIAL
901 BATTERY STREET
SUITE 212
SAN FRANCISCO, CA 94111

901 BATTERY STREET
SUITE 212
SAN FRANCISCO, CA 94111
TEL. 415.986.8014
FAX. 415.986.7649

Client:
Hartman Aviation
Nature of Business:
Leasing and selling small aircraft
Design Firm:
Woods + Woods
Art Director:
Paul Woods
Designer:
Paul Woods

Client:
Hope Cottage Adoption Center
Nature of Business:
Center advocating enlightened adoptions
Design Firm:
RBMM/The Richards Group
Art Director:
Pamela Chang
Designer:
Pamela Chang

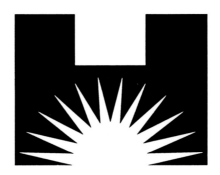

Client:
Field Harbor Ventures
Nature of Business:
Parking facility management
Design Firm:
Three Communication Design
Art Director:
Three Communication Design
Designer:
Three Communication Design

**Field Harbor
Condominium Parking**

165 Field Boulevard
Chicago, Illinois 60601

Direct Mail to:
400 East Randolph Suite 500
Chicago, Illinois 60601

Telephone 312-938-8989

Chicago's First Independent
Condominium Parking Facility

**Field Harbor
Condominium Parking**

165 Field Boulevard
Chicago, Illinois 60601

Direct Mail to:
400 East Randolph Suite 500
Chicago, Illinois 60601

John F. Kretchmar
Project Director
Telephone 312-938-8989

**Field Harbor
Condominium Parking**

165 Field Boulevard
Chicago, Illinois 60601

Direct Mail to:
400 East Randolph Suite 500
Chicago, Illinois 60601

Chicago's First Independent
Condominium Parking Facility

Client:
GTE External Communications
Nature of Business:
Telecommunications
Design Firm:
GTE Graphic Communications
Art Director:
Michael Meade
Designer:
Michael Meade

Client:
Harris Chair Center
Nature of Business:
Chair manufacturing
Design Firm:
Supon Design Group
Art Director:
Supon Phornirunlit
Designer:
Dianne Cook

Client:
Halo Lighting, A Division of Cooper Lighting
Nature of Business:
Track and recessed fixtures
Design Firm:
VSA Partners, Inc.
Art Director:
James Koval
Designer:
James Koval

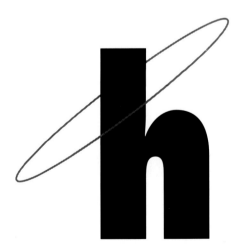

Client:
GTE External Communications
Nature of Business:
Telecommunications
Design Firm:
GTE Graphic Communications
Art Director:
Michael Meade
Designer:
Michael Meade
Printer:
Color-Tech Graphics Inc.

Effective

Communications:

Turning the Power On

1991 External/Internal

Communications

Conference

1991 External/Internal

Communications

Conference

Notes

Client:
R. Kamnatnik Design Ltd.
Nature of Business:
Graphic design
Design Firm:
R. Kamnatnik Design
Art Director:
R. Kamnatnik
Designer:
R. Kamnatnik

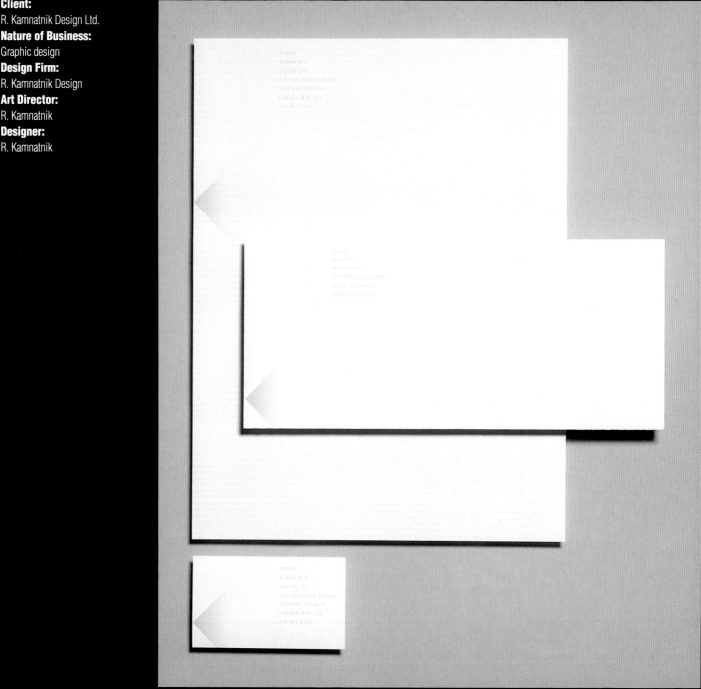

Client:
INFA Telecom Asia Ltd.
Nature of Business:
Digital communications
Design Firm:
Kan Tai-keung Design & Associates Ltd.
Art Director:
Kan Tai-keung, Freeman Lau Siu Hong
Designer:
Benny Au Tak Shing
Creative Director:
Kan Tai-keung

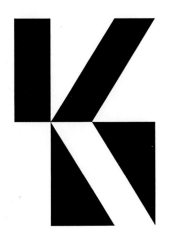

Client:
Champion International
Nature of Business:
Paper manufacturing
Design Firm:
Pentagram Design
Art Director:
Woody Pirtle
Designer:
Woody Pirtle, John Klotnia

Client:
Laser Master Ltd.
Nature of Business:
Karaoke laser disk authorized distribution
Design Firm:
Kan Tai-keung Design & Associates Ltd.
Art Director:
Freeman Lau Siu Hong, Clement Yick Tat Wa
Designer:
Clement Yick Tat Wa
Creative Director:
Kan Tai-keung

Client:
Montserrat Sarria
Nature of Business:
Antiques
Design Firm:
Sonsoles Llorens Design
Art Director:
Sonsoles Llorens
Designer:
Sonsoles Llorens

Client:
Insight Development Corporation
Nature of Business:
Printing utility software
Design Firm:
The Stephenz Group
Art Director:
Stephanie Paulson
Designer:
Phillip Kim

Client:
Print Northwest
Nature of Business:
Lithography
Design Firm:
Hornall Anderson Design Works
Art Director:
Jack Anderson
Designer:
Jack Anderson, Heidi Hatlestad

Client:
Print Northwest
Nature of Business:
Lithography
Design Firm:
Hornall Anderson Design Works
Art Director:
Jack Anderson
Designer:
Jack Anderson, Heidi Hatlestad

Client:
Martha Burns
Nature of Business:
Interior and textile design
Design Firm:
Pentagram Design
Art Director:
Michael Bierut
Designer:
Michael Bierut

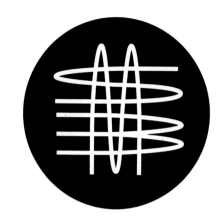

Client:
Never Never Adrian
Nature of Business:
Women's sportswear
Design Firm:
Studio Seireeni
Art Director:
Richard Seireeni
Designer:
Brian Birchfield

Client:
Louise Owen III
Nature of Business:
Watchmaking
Design Firm:
Supon Design Group
Art Director:
Supon Phornirunlit
Designer:
Dave Prescott

Nevernever Adrian
Division of Amarotico GmbH
Zieglerstraße 10 · Postfach 12 13
D-6200 Wiesbaden 1

Tel.: 06 11 - 56 10 74
Fax: 06 11 - 56 21 30

ADRIAN
RUNHOF
Managing
Director

Nevernever Adrian
Division of Amarotico GmbH
Zieglerstraße 10 · Postfach 12 13
D-8200 Wiesbaden 1

Tel.: 06 11 - 56 10 74
Fax: 06 11 - 56 21 30

Client:
Never Never Adrian
Nature of Business:
Women's sportswear
Design Firm:
Studio Seireeni

Client:
Planex Oy
Nature of Business:
Exhibition stand design and fitting
Design Firm:
Viktorno Design Oy
Art Director:
Viktor Kaltala
Designer:
Viktor Kaltala

Client:
Royal Viking Line
Nature of Business:
International cruise line
Design Firm:
Pentagram Design, Inc.
Art Director:
Neil Shakery
Designer:
Neil Shakery

Client:
Corning Incorporated
Nature of Business:
Total Quality/Industrial products
Design Firm:
Michael Orr & Associates
Art Director:
Michael Orr
Designer:
Michael Orr, Michael Callahan

Client:
Rumble
Nature of Business:
Musicians
Design Firm:
RBMM
Art Director:
Luis D. Acevedo
Designer:
Luis D. Acevedo

Client:
Radical Rye Sandwich Shop
Nature of Business:
Restaurant
Design Firm:
Planet Design Company
Art Director:
Kevin Wade, Dana Lytle
Designer:
Kevin Wade

Client:
Elio Sellino Editore
Nature of Business:
Publishing
Design Firm:
Esseblu
Art Director:
Susanna Vallebona
Designer:
Susanna Vallebona

Client:
Scherer, Sutherland & Associates
Video Productions Inc.
Nature of Business:
Video and television presentations production
Design Firm:
Bruce E. Morgan Graphic Design
Art Director:
Bruce E. Morgan
Designer:
Bruce E. Morgan

ELIO SELLINO EDITORE   20135 Milano, vl. Cirene 15   Elio Sellino Editore srl   CCIAA Milano 1361753

Tel. 02/55193662, 55193677   Capitale Sociale L. 95.000.000   C.F. e Part. IVA 10301010152

Fax 02/55193677   Trib. Mi. 314144 v. 7865 f. 44

ELIO SELLINO   20135 Milano   Elio Sellino Ed. srl
EDITORE   Viale Cirene, 15   Cod. Fisc e P. IVA
Tel. 02/55193662   10301010152
Fax 02/55193677

Elio Sellino

ELIO SELLINO EDITORE

Client:
Elio Sellino Editore
Nature of Business:
Publishing
Design Firm:
Esseblu
Art Director:
Susanna Vallebona
Designer:
Susanna Vallebona

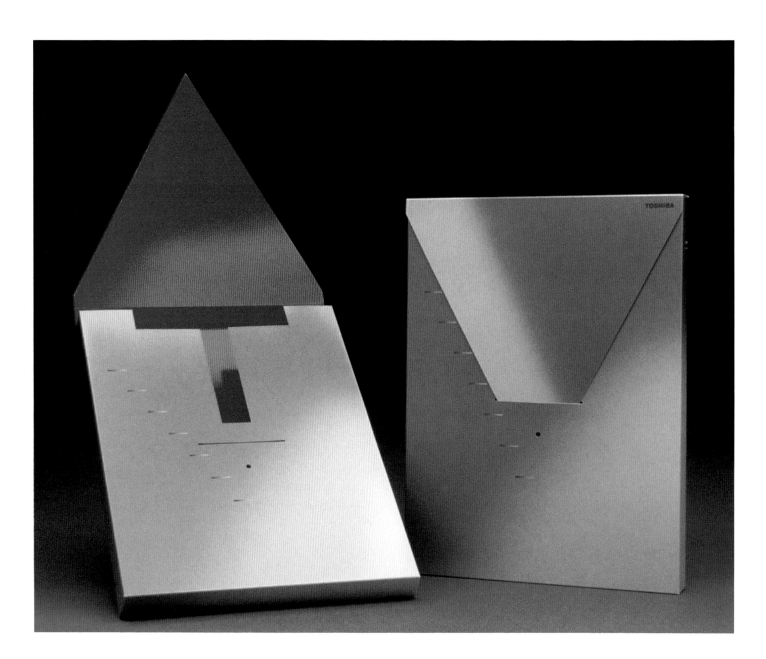

Client:
Toshiba America Medical Systems
Nature of Business:
Medical equipment manufacturing
Design Firm:
Bruce Yelaska Design
Art Director:
Bruce Yelaska
Designer:
Bruce Yelaska

Client:
Hong Kong Telecom
Nature of Business:
Telecommunications
Design Firm:
Landor Associates
Art Director:
Byron Jacobs
Designer:
Byron Jacobs

Client:
Ulman Paper Bag Company
Nature of Business:
Bag manufacturing
Design Firm:
Supon Design Group
Art Director:
Supon Phornirunlit
Designer:
Supon Phornirunlit

Client:
Union Gas
Nature of Business:
Utility
Design Firm:
Gottschalk+Ash International
Art Director:
Stuart Ash
Designer:
Stuart Ash

Client:
Union Energy
Nature of Business:
Utility
Design Firm:
Gottschalk+Ash International
Art Director:
Stuart Ash
Designer:
Stuart Ash

Client:
Vita Mills Inc.
Nature of Business:
Natural, whole-grain cereal and bread manufacturing
Design Firm:
Siren Design Studios
Art Director:
Jim Yue
Designer:
David Cheng

Client:
Valuation Services Ltd.
Nature of Business:
Gem testing laboratory and jewelry appraising
Design Firm:
Byron Jacobs
Art Director:
Byron Jacobs
Designer:
Byron Jacobs

V A L U A T I O N   S E R V I C E S

V A L U A T I O N   S E R V I C E S

V A L U A T I O N   S E R V I C E S

Judith Grieder Jacobs, G.G., F.G.A.
Gemmologist

Valuation Services Limited
P.O. Box 11996 General Post Office
Hong Kong
Telephone: (852) 810-6640
Fax: (852) 522-4545.

Valuation Services Limited
D-3, 11 MacDonnell Road
Hong Kong
Telephone: 810-6640
Fax: (852) 522-4545

Client:
Valuation Services Ltd.
Nature of Business:

Client:
Buena Vista College
Nature of Business:
College
Design Firm:
Sayles Graphic Design
Art Director:
John Sayles
Designer:
John Sayles

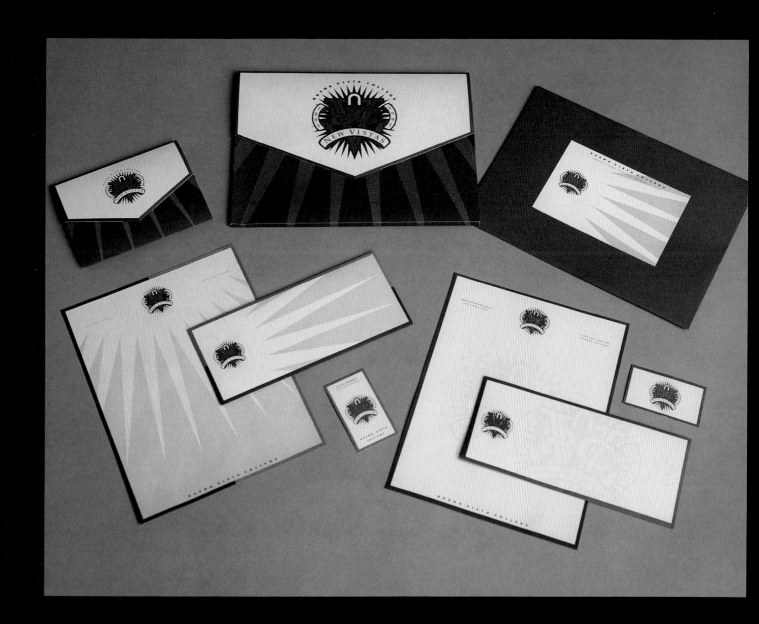

Client:
Buena Vista College
Nature of Business:
College
Design Firm:
Sayles Graphic Design
Art Director:
John Sayles
Designer:
John Sayles

WILLINGTOWN CONSTRUCTION

P.O. BOX 4
YORKLYN,
DELAWARE
19736

3 0 2 • 2 3 9 • 1 8 0 0

WILLINGTOWN CONSTRUCTION

P.O. BOX 4
YORKLYN,
DELAWARE 19736

WILLINGTOWN CONSTRUCTION

P.O. BOX 4
YORKLYN,
DELAWARE 19736

3 0 2 • 2 3 9 • 1 8 0 0

Chris Sanger

Client:
Hornall Anderson Design Works
Nature of Business:
10 Year Anniversary/Graphic design firm
Design Firm:
Hornall Anderson Design Works
Art Director:
Jack Anderson
Designer:
Jack Anderson, John Hornall, David Bates, Paula Cox,
Lian Ng, Leo Raymundo, Jani Drewfs

VAUGHN

WEDEEN

CREATIVE INC

407

RIO GRANDE NW   TEL

ALBUQUERQUE   505 243 4000   EMMA E ROBERTS

NEW MEXICO   FAX

USA 87104   505 247 9856

VAUGHN

WEDEEN

CREATIVE

INC.

VAUGHN

WEDEEN

CREATIVE

INC

407

RIO GRANDE

NW

ALBUQUERQUE

NEW MEXICO

USA

87104

TEL

505 243 4000

FAX

505 247 9856

Client:
Vaughn/Wedeen Creative
Nature of Business:
Design
Design Firm:
Vaughn/Wedeen Creative
Art Director:
Dan Flynn, Rick Vaughn,
Steve Wedeen
Designer:
Dan Flynn

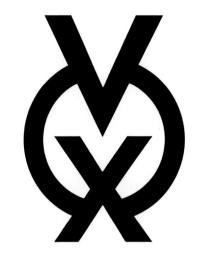

Client:
VOX Records
Nature of Business:
Recording
Design Firm:
PolyGram Records
Art Director:
Margery Greenspan
Designer:
Giulio Turturro
Creative Director:
Michael Bays

Client:
Whaley Excavating Inc.
Nature of Business:
Excavating and backhoe work
Design Firm:
Grand Pré and Whaley, Ltd.
Art Director:
Kevin Whaley
Designer:
Kevin Whaley

Client:
Entrekin/Zucco
Nature of Business:
Advertising
Design Firm:
Frank D'Astolfo Design
Art Director:
Frank D'Astolfo
Designer:
Frank D'Astolfo

Client:
Victoria Bermejo
Nature of Business:
Copywriting
Design Firm:
Sonsoles Llorens Design
Art Director:
Sonsoles Llorens
Designer:
Sonsoles Llorens

Client:
The Artists' Gallery
Nature of Business:
Art exhibition
Design Firm:
Richard Lee Heffner Design
Art Director:
Richard Lee Heffner
Designer:
Richard Lee Heffner

Client:
The Kibbe Group Inc.
Nature of Business:
Creative business communications consortium
Design Firm:
Bhote-Siegel Design
Art Director:
Shenaya Bhote-Siegel
Designer:
Shenaya Bhote-Siegel, Wendy Blattner
Illustrator:
Wendy Blattner

Client:
Value Added Design Pty. Ltd.
Nature of Business:
Graphic design
Design Firm:
Value Added Design Pty. Ltd.
Art Director:
Heather Towns-Cook
Designer:
Heather Towns-Cook

3385 M North Arlington Heights Rd.
Arlington Heights, Illinois 60004

Creative Business Communications

THE KIBBE GROUP INC

3385 M North
Arlington Heights Rd.
Arlington Heights,
Illinois 60004
708.392.7800
708.392.7808 fax

Thomas G. Kibbe
President

 3385 M North Arlington Heights Rd. ● Arlington Heights, Illinois 60004 ● 708.392.7800 ● 708.392.7808 fax

Client:
The Kibbe Group Inc.
Nature of Business:
Creative business communications consortium
Design Firm:
Bhote-Siegel Design

Client:
Good Pictures
Nature of Business:
Video production
Design Firm:
Morla Design, Inc.
Art Director:
Jennifer Morla
Designer:
Jennifer Morla, Sharrie Brooks

Client:
National Travelers Life
Nature of Business:
Insurance
Design Firm:
Sayles Graphic Design
Art Director:
John Sayles
Designer:
John Sayles

Client:
Candid Signs Pte. Ltd.
Nature of Business:
Signage fabrication
Design Firm:
Design Objectives Pte. Ltd.
Art Director:
Ronnie S.C. Tan
Designer:
Ng Chin Joon

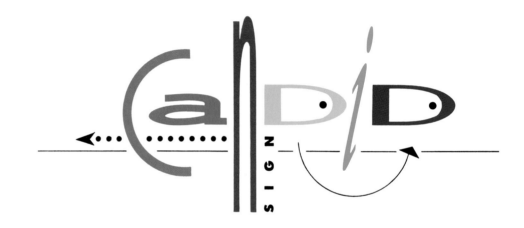

Client:
Literal Corporation
Nature of Business:
Manufacturing of optical disk drives
Design Firm:
Volan Design Associates
Art Director:
Michele Braverman
Designer:
Michele Braverman

Client:
Da Vinci Groep
Nature of Business:
Information technology consulting
Design Firm:
Samenwerkende Ontwerpers
Art Director:
André Toet
Designer:
Hans Meiboom

Client:
Laines Furnishings
Nature of Business:
Fabric distribution
Design Firm:
FHA Design
Art Director:
Richard Henderson
Designer:
Richard Henderson, Lee McCartney

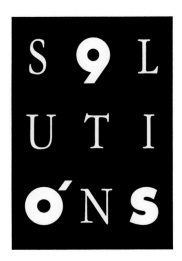

Client:
Apple Computer, Inc.
Nature of Business:
Computer manufacturing
Design Firm:
Pentagram Design
Art Director:
Woody Pirtle
Designer:
Woody Pirtle, Libby Carton

Client:
20/20 4sight
Nature of Business:
Recording
Design Firm:
PolyGram Records
Art Director:
Margery Greenspan
Designer:
Giulio Turturro
Creative Director:
Michael Bays

Client:
Pacific Dunlop Pty. Ltd.
Nature of Business:
Clothing
Design Firm:
Brian Sadgrove & Associates
Art Director:
Brian Sadgrove
Designer:
Brian Sadgrove

Client:
Connect Computer Company
Nature of Business:
Computer networking
Design Firm:
Larsen Design Office, Inc.
Art Director:
Tim Larsen
Designer:
Marc Kundmann

Client:
Active Voice
Nature of Business:
Manufacturing and distribution of
voice-messaging equipment
Design Firm:
Hornall Anderson Design Works
Art Director:
Jack Anderson
Designer:
Jack Anderson, Julia LaPine,
David Bates, Mary Hermes, Lian Ng

Client:
Neo Technics Pty. Ltd.
Nature of Business:
Product design and development consulting
Design Firm:
Emery Vincent Associates
Art Director:
Emery Vincent Associates
Designer:
Emery Vincent Associates

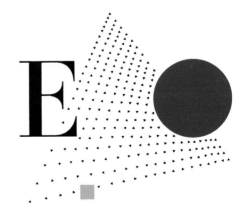

CITRON
Santa Monica

Citron Clothing
1611 Montana Avenue
Santa Monica, Ca 90403

CITRON
Santa Monica

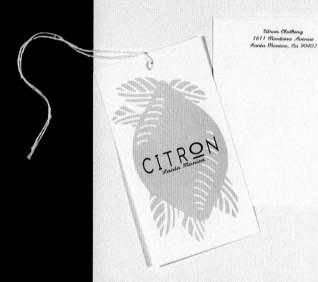

Citron Clothing, 1611 Montana Avenue, Santa Monica

CITRON
Santa Monica

AVIVA HOLMAN

Ca 90403 Telephone (310) 458-6089 Fax (310) 453-4076

Citron Clothing
1611 Montana Avenue
Santa Monica, Ca 90403
Telephone (310) 458-6089
Fax (310) 453-4076

Client:
Clos St. Thomas
Nature of Business:
Winemaking
Design Firm:
Akagi Design
Art Director:
Doug Akagi
Designer:
Doug Akagi, Kimberly Lentz-Powell

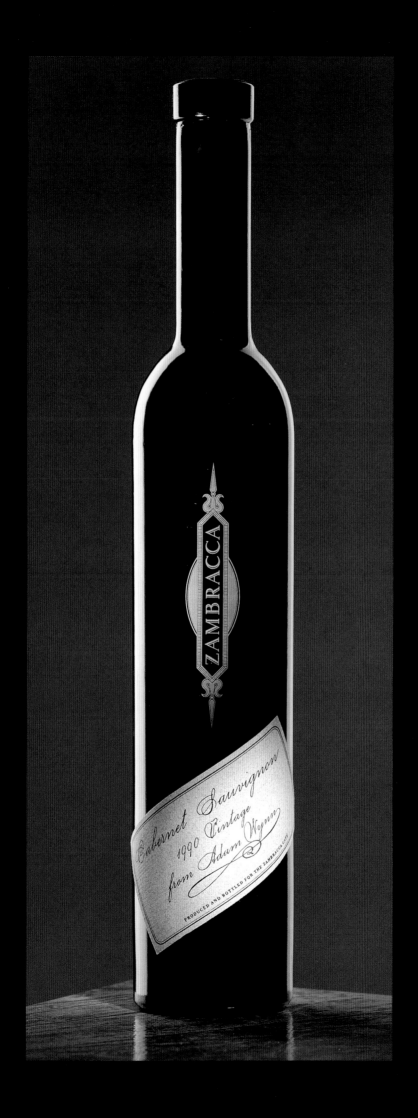

Client:
The Zambracca Cafe
Nature of Business:
Restaurant
Design Firm:
Barrie Tucker Design Pty. Ltd.
Art Director:
Barrie Tucker
Designer:
Barrie Tucker, Andrew Davies

65

Client:

Ciao Bella Gelato Co.

Nature of Business:

Gelato and sorbet manufacturing

Design Firm:

Spark Design, Inc.

Designer:

Walter Clarke, Michael Boland,

Kerri Konik

Client:
System Action
Nature of Business:
Clothing retailing
Design Firm:
Sonsoles Llorens Design
Art Director:
Sonsoles Llorens
Designer:
Sonsoles Llorens

Client:

Texpro Textile Productions

Nature of Business:

Textile design and manufacturing

Design Firm:

Mammoliti Chan Design

Art Director:

Tony Mammoliti

Designer:

Tony Mammoliti, Chwee Kuan Chan

Client:

The Light Car Company Ltd.

Nature of Business:

Car manufacturing and designing

Design Firm:

The Team

Art Director:

Richard Ward

Designer:

Richard Ward

Handlettering:

Paul Gray

Client:

Micro-Boutique Inc.

Nature of Business:

Authorized Apple dealer

Design Firm:

K-O

Art Director:

K-O

Designer:

K-O

Client:
Adelphi Hotel
Nature of Business:
Hospitality
Design Firm:
Emery Vincent Associates
Art Director:
Emery Vincent Associates
Designer:
Emery Vincent Associates

Client:
Soma
Nature of Business:
Computer and electronic equipment
Design Firm:
Gottschalk+Ash International
Art Director:
Stuart Ash
Designer:
Heather Lafleur

Client:
Micro Storage Systems Inc.
Nature of Business:
Digital storage equipment
Design Firm:
Volan Design Associates
Art Director:
Justin Deister
Designer:
Justin Deister

Client:
General Information (HotLine)
Nature of Business:
Software product
Design Firm:
Hornall Anderson Design Works
Art Director:
Jack Anderson
Designer:
Jack Anderson, Julia LaPine, Brian O'Neill

E X O S

E X O S

Lewis I. Nathan
Software Engineer

EXOS Inc.

2A Gill Street
Woburn, MA 01801

617.933.0022 tel
617.933.0303 fax

E X O S

EXOS Inc.

2A Gill Street
Woburn, MA 01801

EXOS Inc.

2A Gill Street
Woburn, MA 01801

617.933.0022 tel
617.933.0303 fax

Client:
ki Research
Nature of Business:
Computer software
Design Firm:
Supon Design Group
Art Director:
Supon Phornirunlit
Designer:
Andrew Dolan

Client:
Zoë Restaurant
Nature of Business:
Restaurant
Design Firm:
John Kneapler Design
Art Director:
John Kneapler
Designer:
John Kneapler, Matt Waldman

Client:
Chex International Ltd.
Nature of Business:
Fashion boutique
Design Firm:
Kan Tai-keung Design & Associates Ltd.
Art Director:
Freeman Lau Siu Hong
Designer:
Freeman Lau Siu Hong
Creative Director:
Kan Tai-keung

Client:
ki Research
Nature of Business:
Computer software
Design Firm:
Supon Design Group
Art Director:
Supon Phornirunlit
Designer:
Andrew Dolan

Client:
Museo de Arte Contemporáneo de Monterrey,
Monterrey, México
Nature of Business:
Contemporary art museum
Design Firm:
Lance Wyman Ltd.
Art Director:
Lance Wyman
Designer:
Lance Wyman, Denise Guerra

Client:
Wisdom Health Care Initiatives
Nature of Business:
Health care consulting
Design Firm:
Gottschalk+Ash International
Art Director:
Peter Steiner
Designer:
Michael Wou

Client:
Tony Geeves & Associates for APPM
Nature of Business:
Paper manufacturing
Design Firm:
David Lancashire Design
Art Director:
David Lancashire
Designer:
David Lancashire

Client:
Tony Geeves & Associates for APPM
Nature of Business:
Paper manufacturing
Design Firm:
David Lancashire Design
Art Director:
David Lancashire
Designer:

Client:
Vaughn/Wedeen Creative
Nature of Business:
Design
Design Firm:
Vaughn/Wedeen Creative
Art Director:
Rick Vaughn, Steve Wedeen, Dan Flynn
Designer:
Dan Flynn

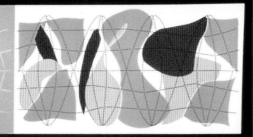

Client:
Mon Bar
Nature of Business:
Beer and tapas bar
Design Firm:
Sonsoles Llorens Design
Art Director:
Sonsoles Llorens
Designer:
Sonsoles Llorens

Client:
Laughing Dog Creative, Inc.
Nature of Business:
Graphic design
Design Firm:
Laughing Dog Creative, Inc.
Art Director:
Joy Panos
Designer:
Joy Panos
Creative Director:
Frank E.E. Grubich
Printing:
Ultra Graphics Litho, Inc.

Client:
Pacific Motion Pictures
Nature of Business:
Movie production and direction
Design Firm:
Fuze Inc.
Art Director:
Ross Patrick
Designer:

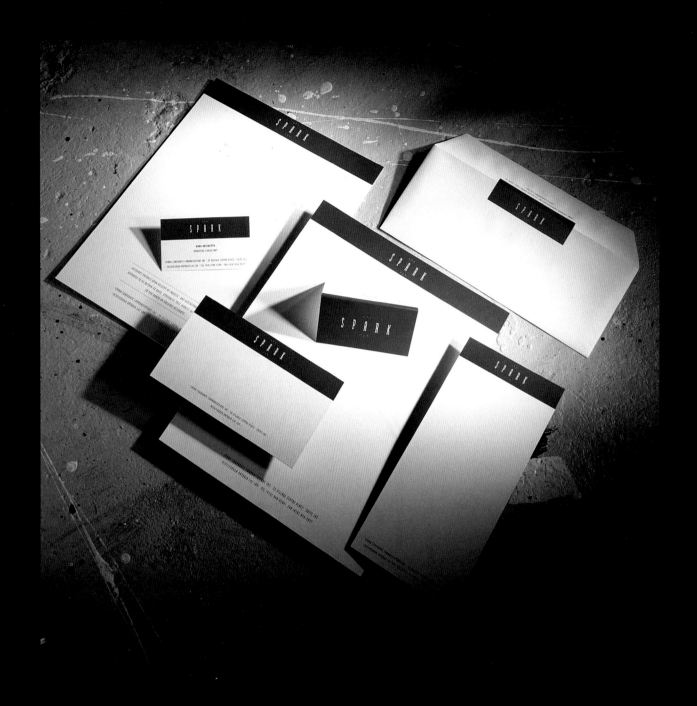

Client:
Spark Corporate Communications
Nature of Business:
Corporate communications
Design Firm:
Rushton Green and Grossutti
Art Director:
Rosanna D'Agostino
Designer:
Rosanna D'Agostino

Client:
Micrographics
Nature of Business:
Computer software and hardware
Design Firm:
mpd/Michael Pagliuco Design
Art Director:
Michael Pagliuco
Designer:
Michael Pagliuco
Photography:
Charles Steele
B/W Print:
Ron Gordon
Handcoloring:
Julia Ryan

Client:
Eureka Farm Produce
Nature of Business:
Condiment, oil, and jam manufacturing
Design Firm:
David Lancashire Design
Art Director:
David Lancashire
Designer:
David Lancashire
Finished Art:
A. Aniulis
Lettering:
G. Fawcett

WALLACE JAMES SHAW
56 PELHAM LANE
WILTON, CONNECTICUT 06897
TEL (203) 761-1176
NY TEL (914) 632-1774

WALLACE JAMES SHAW
56 PELHAM LANE
WILTON, CONNECTICUT 06897
TEL (203) 761-1176
NY TEL (914) 632-1774

WALLACE JAMES SHAW
56 PELHAM LANE
WILTON, CONNECTICUT 06897

Client:
Shaw Nautical
Nature of Business:
Professional woodworking
Design Firm:
Wallace Church Associates, Inc.
Art Director:
Stanley Church
Designer:
Joe Cuticone
Illustrator:
Joe Cuticone

Design Firm:
VSA Partners, Inc.
Art Director:
James Koval
Designer:
James Koval
Illustrator:
Mary Flock

PEABERRY COFFEE, LTD
1685 SOUTH COLORADO BLVD., UNIT C
DENVER, COLORADO 80222
303.756.4111

PEABERRY COFFEE, LTD
1685 SOUTH COLORADO BLVD, UNIT C
DENVER, COLORADO 80222
303.756.4111

Client:
Peaberry Coffee, Ltd.
Nature of Business:
Retail coffee franchising
Design Firm:
VSA Partners, Inc.
Art Director:
James Koval
Designer:
James Koval
Illustrator:
Mary Flock

Client:
Peaberry Coffee, Ltd.
Nature of Business:
Retail coffee franchising
Design Firm:
VSA Partners, Inc.
Art Director:
James Koval
Designer:
James Koval
Illustrator:
Mary Flock

Client:
Woolo Co.
Nature of Business:
Clothing manufacturing
Design Firm:
Supon Design Group
Art Director:
Supon Phornirunlit
Designer:
Richard Lee Heffner

Client:
The Oakford-Melbourne
Nature of Business:
24-hour restaurant within 5-star hotel
Design Firm:
Annette Harcus Design Pty. Ltd.
Art Director:
Annette Harcus
Designer:
Annette Harcus, Sean Gibbs

THE BUFFET

PLANTATIONS FEATURES AN EVERCHANGING BUFFET THROUGHOUT THE DAY AND EVENING. USING THE FRESHEST MARKET PRODUCE AVAILABLE, OUR TALENTED CHEFS HAVE CREATED A CULINARY FEAST USING A COMBINATION OF INGREDIENTS FROM THE EAST AND WEST, TO SURPRISE THE MOST DISCERNING OF DINERS AND SATISFY THE HEARTIEST OF APPETITES.

Our staff will be pleased to introduce to
you today's selection at
$27.00 per person

ENTRÉES

Oysters in half shells served natural
Half Dozen $14.00 One Dozen $19.50
(Our Chef will be pleased to make your choice of Kilpatrick, Mornay, or any of your preferences)

Salad of assorted lettuce with Chicken, apples, and mushrooms
$9.50

Angelhair pasta with scallops and tiger prawns
$12.50

Salad of seafood with frisée salad and corn chips
$13.00

SOUPS

Pumpkin and coconut soup
$5.00

Consommé of Chicken with finely chopped vegetables
$6.00

LIGHT SNACKS & SALADS

Trio of opened-faced sandwiches, with your choice of ham, salami, tuna,
avocado, turkey, or cheese
$9.50
Plantations Triple Decker
$12.50
Virginia ham sliced from the bone, served with spicy mustard sauce
$10.50
Beef carpaccio with antipasto
$13.50
Slivers of smoked salmon with selected traditional garnishes
$19.00
Spicy lamb satay on a melon and chilli coulis
$13.00

MAIN COURSES

_____ fillet with your choice of sauce

Client:
The Oakford-Melbourne
Nature of Business:
24-hour restaurant within 5-star hotel
Design Firm:
Annette Harcus Design Pty. Ltd.
Art Director:
Annette Harcus
Designer:
Annette Harcus, Sean Gibbs

Client:
Eagle Lake on Orcas Island
Nature of Business:
Development
Design Firm:
Hornall Anderson Design Works
Art Director:
Julia LaPine
Designer:
Julia LaPine, Denise Weir

Client:
California Grill/Euro Disney Resorts
Nature of Business:
California Grill
Design Firm:
David Carter Graphic Design
Art Director:
Gary Lobue, Jr.
Designer:
Gary Lobue, Jr.

Client:
Food Services of America
Nature of Business:
Nobody Provides Better Service/
Institutional food distribution
Design Firm:
Hornall Anderson Design Works
Art Director:
Jack Anderson
Designer:
Jack Anderson, Mike Courtney,
David Bates

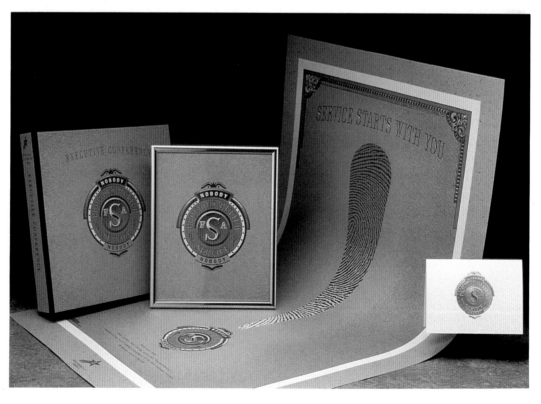

Client:
Empire Hotel
Nature of Business:
Hospitality
Design Firm:
Pentagram Design
Art Director:
Michael Gericke, Peter Harrison
Designer:
Michael Gericke

Client:
Bullwhackers
Nature of Business:
Restaurant and casino
Design Firm:
Bright & Associates
Art Director:
Keith Bright
Designer:
Raymond Wood

Client:
Richard Louis Cosmetics Ltd.
Nature of Business:
All-natural cosmetics
Design Firm:
Anagram Design Group Inc.
Art Director:
Carmine Vecchio
Designer:
Carmine Vecchio

Client:
Kaso
Nature of Business:
Jewelry and accessories
Design Firm:
John Kneapler Design
Art Director:
John Kneapler
Designer:
John Kneapler, Matt Waldman

Client:
Evenson Design
Nature of Business:
Graphic design
Design Firm:
Evenson Design Group
Art Director:
Stan Evenson
Designer:
Stan Evenson

Client:
Blackthorne Capital Inc.
Nature of Business:
Stocks and commodities trading and investing
Design Firm:
Bhote-Siegel Design Inc.
Art Director:
Shenaya Bhote-Siegel
Designer:
Shenaya Bhote-Siegel, Donna McGrath
Illustrator:
Donna McGrath

Client:
Buchan Communications Pty. Ltd.
Nature of Business:
Public relations consulting
Design Firm:
Brian Sadgrove & Associates
Art Director:
Brian Sadgrove
Designer:
Brian Sadgrove

Client:
Eaglemoor
Nature of Business:
Golf clothier
Design Firm:
Hornall Anderson Design Works
Art Director:
Jack Anderson
Designer:
Jack Anderson, Mary Hermes, David Bates

BLACKTHORNE™

Managed Commodity Accounts

BLACKTHORNE™

Blackthorne Capital, Inc.
3065 Blackthorne Lane
Riverwoods, Illinois 60015
708.945.5125
708.945.7007 Fax

Timothy Morge
President

Managed Commodity Accounts

BLACKTHORNE™

Managed Commodity Accounts

Blackthorne Capital, Inc.
3065 Blackthorne Lane
Riverwoods, Illinois 60015

Blackthorne Capital, Inc.   3065 Blackthorne Lane   Riverwoods, Illinois 60015   708.945.5125   708.945.7007 Fax

Client:
Blackthorne Capital Inc.
Nature of Business:
Stocks and commodities trading and investing
Design Firm:
Bhote-Siegel Design Inc.
Art Director:
Shenaya Bhote-Siegel
Designer:
Shenaya Bhote-Siegel, Donna McGrath
Illustrator:
Donna McGrath

Client:
Speedware Corporation
Nature of Business:
Software development
Design Firm:
Rushton Green and Grossutti
Art Director:
Marcello Grossutii
Designer:
Gino Ciarmela

Client:
Compass Airlines Pty. Ltd.
Nature of Business:
Airline
Design Firm:
Brian Sadgrove & Associates
Art Director:
Brian Sadgrove
Designer:
Brian Sadgrove

Compass

Client:
Viewer's Choice
Nature of Business:
Television
Design Firm:
Gottschalk+Ash International
Art Director:
Stuart Ash
Designer:
Heather Lafleur

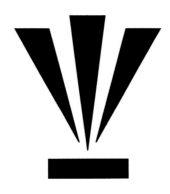

VIEWER'S CHOICE

Client:
Olive Restaurant
Nature of Business:
Restaurant
Design Firm:
Studio Seireeni
Art Director:
Richard Seireeni
Designer:
Romane Cameron
Creative Director:
Sean MacPhearson

O L I V E

Sean K. MacPherson

119 SOUTH FAIRFAX
LOS ANGELES
CALIFORNIA 90036
PHONE 213 939 2001
FAX 213 934 1099

119 SOUTH FAIRFAX LOS ANGELES CALIFORNIA 90036 PHONE 213 939 2001 FAX 213 934 1099

Client:
Hotel Okura
Nature of Business:
Hospitality
Design Firm:
UCI
Art Director:
Ryo Urano
Designer:
Tracy Asari

Client:
Older Persons Planning Office
Nature of Business:
Benefits card for senior citizens
Design Firm:
FHA Design
Art Director:
Richard Henderson
Designer:
Richard Henderson, Marcus Lee

Client:
Deja Shoe Corporation
Nature of Business:
Casual shoes from recycled materials
Design Firm:
Bielenberg Design
Art Director:
John Bielenberg
Designer:
Kathy Warinner

Client:
Plastic
Nature of Business:
Music contracting
Design Firm:
Sonsoles Llorens Design
Art Director:
Sonsoles Llorens
Designer:
Sonsoles Llorens

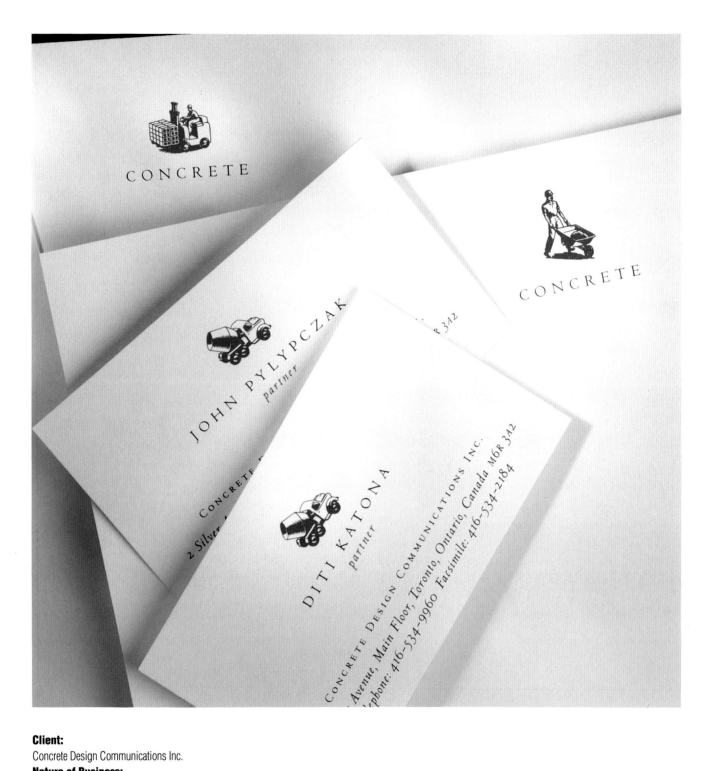

Client:
Concrete Design Communications Inc.
Nature of Business:
Graphic design
Design Firm:
Concrete Design Communications Inc.
Art Director:
John Pylypczak, Diti Katona
Designer:
John Pylypczak, Diti Katona
Illustrator:
Ross MacDonald

FREEMAN

COMMUNICATIONS

11 GLOUCESTER

STREET

TORONTO

ONTARIO

M4Y 1L8

T 416/967/6970

F 416/967/5459

Corporate
Graphic
Design &
Management

A Division of Type Art Inc.

FREEMAN

COMMUNICATIONS

11 GLOUCESTER

STREET

TORONTO

ONTARIO

M4Y 1L8

Corporate
Graphic
Design &
Management

FREEMAN

COMMUNICATIONS

11 GLOUCESTER

STREET

TORONTO

ONTARIO

M4Y 1L8

T 416/967/6970

F 416/967/5459

Corporate
Graphic
Design &
Management

BERT FREEMAN GDC
*President /
Creative Director*

Client:
Freeman Communications
Nature of Business:
Graphic design
Design Firm:
Freeman Communications
Art Director:
Bert Freeman
Designer:

Client:
Art Directors Club of Metropolitan Washington
Nature of Business:
Design professionals association
Design Firm:
Supon Design Group
Art Director:
Supon Phornirunlit
Designer:
Supon Phornirunlit
Photographer:
Barry Myers

HOUSE OF QUALITY

HOWARD PAPER MILLS
5088 VERMACK RD
DUNWOODY, GEORGIA 30338

PHONE/FAX: 1-404-594-9695
WATS: 1-800-543-5010

HOWARD PAPER MILLS
521 JACKSON AVE
GLENCOE, ILLINOIS 60022

Peter K. Wittman
Business Communication Papers

PHONE: 1-708-719-5740
FAX: 1-312-419-0815

HOUSE OF QUALITY

HOWARD PAPER MILLS
3690 ALDER LANE
PASADENA, CALIFORNIA 91107

HOUSE OF QUALITY

Client:
Howard Paper Mills
Nature of Business:
Papermaking/printing
Design Firm:
Grand Design
Art Director:

Designer:

Client:
Dallas Children's Advocacy Center League
Nature of Business:
Charity
Design Firm:
RBMM
Art Director:
Horacio Cobos, Dick Mitchell
Designer:
Horacio Cobos

Client:
Sequoia Lodge/Euro Disney Resorts
Nature of Business:
Hospitality
Design Firm:
David Carter Graphic Design
Art Director:
David Brashier
Designer:
David Brashier

Client:
St. Hedwigs Senior Center
Nature of Business:
Senior center for elderly day care
Design Firm:
Delmarva Power - Visual Communications
Art Director:
Susan McGuane
Designer:
Susan North, Paul Stecca
Illustrator:
Shokie Bragg

Client:
Innerspace Commercial Furnishings Pty. Ltd.
Nature of Business:
Commercial furnishings
Design Firm:
Emery Vincent Associates
Art Director:
Emery Vincent Associates
Designer:
Emery Vincent Associates

Client:
ITT Sheraton Corporation
Nature of Business:
Restaurant at Sheraton Manhattan Hotel
Design Firm:
Coco Raynes/Graphics, Inc.
Art Director:
Coco Raynes
Designer:
Kevin Sheehan

Client:
AG Communication Systems
Nature of Business:
Promotional logo/Graphic design
Design Firm:
AG Communication Systems Design Group
Art Director:
Jeffrey Moss
Designer:
Jeffrey Moss

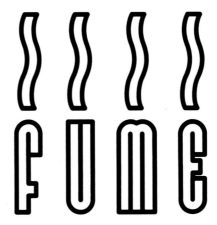

Client:
Dr. Jonathan Hartley
Nature of Business:
Dentistry
Design Firm:
Brian Sadgrove & Associates
Art Director:
Brian Sadgrove
Designer:
Brian Sadgrove

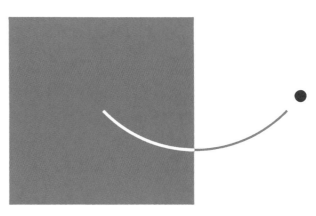

DR JONATHAN S HARTLEY
DENTISTRY

Client:
IBM Switzerland
Nature of Business:
Computers
Design Firm:
BBV
Art Director:
Michael Baviera
Designer:
Michael Baviera

Client:
Fred Eric
Nature of Business:
Chain of taco stands
Design Firm:
Jay Vigon Design & Art Direction
Art Director:
Jay Vigon
Designer:
Jay Vigon

Client:
Dancing Desert Press
Nature of Business:
Publishing
Design Firm:
Vaughn/Wedeen Creative
Art Director:
Rick Vaughn
Designer:
Rick Vaughn

Client:
Bio-Rad Laboratories, Inc.
Nature of Business:
Medical diagnostics and
laboratory instruments
Design Firm:
The Stephenz Group
Art Director:
Stephanie Paulson
Designer:
Phillip Kim
Copywriter:
Barbara Sater
Photographer:
Bill Schwob

Client:
Hotel Santa Fe
Nature of Business:
Hospitality
Design Firm:
Vaughn/Wedeen Creative
Art Director:
Rick Vaughn
Designer:
Dan Flynn

HOTEL SANTA FE

Client:
Acart Graphic Services Inc.
Nature of Business:
Graphic design, communications, and exhibits
Design Firm:
Acart Graphic Services
Art Director:
John Staresinic
Designer:
Ross Gervais
Production Artist:
Ross Gervais

Client:
Hammons Equestrian Center
Nature of Business:
Morgan horse breeding
Design Firm:
Sibley/Peteet Design
Art Director:
Julia Albanesi
Designer:
Julia Albanesi

JOHN STARESINIC
DESIGN DIRECTOR

171 NEPEAN STREET
SUITE 500
OTTAWA, ONTARIO
CANADA K2P 0B4
TEL: (613) 230-7944
FAX: (613) 232-5980

171 NEPEAN STREET
SUITE 500
OTTAWA, ONTARIO
CANADA K2P 0B4
TEL: (613) 230-7944
FAX: (613) 232-5980

COMMUNICATIONS•ADVERTISING•CREATIVE SERVICES•EXHIBITS•COMMUNICATIONS•ADVERTISING•CREATIVE SERVICES•EXHIBITS•COMMUNICATIONS•ADVERTISING•CREATIVE SERVICES•EXHIBITS•COMMUNICATIONS

Client:
The Weller Institute at the Red Hawk Ranch
Nature of Business:
Horse training and designing enterprise
Design Firm:
The Weller Institute for the Cure of Design, Inc.
Art Director:
Don Weller
Designer:
Don Weller

Client:
Biennale Exhibit
Nature of Business:
Exhibits
Design Firm:
Woods + Woods
Art Director:
Paul Woods
Designer:
Paul Woods

Client:
Stardog Records
Nature of Business:
Recording
Design Firm:
PolyGram Records
Art Director:
Michael Bays
Designer:
Mike Klotz
Creative Director:
Michael Bays

114

The
Weller
Institute
For
The
Cure
Of
Design,
Inc.

3091
Fawn
Drive
P O Box
726
Park
City,
Utah
84060

The
Weller
Institute
For
The
Cure
Of
Design,
Inc.

Cha Cha
Weller

3091
Fawn
Drive
P O Box
726
Park
City,
Utah
84060
(801)
649-9859
Fax
(801)
649-4196

3091
Fawn
Drive
P O Box
726
Park
City,
Utah
84060

The
Weller
Institute
For
The
Cure
Of
Design,
Inc.

Please
Call
(801)
649-9859
And
Or
Fax
(801)
649-4196

Home
Office,
Studio
And
Head-
quarters:
Cutting
Horse
Division

Client:
Contor Industries
Nature of Business:
Holding company
Design Firm:
Concrete Design Communications Inc.
Art Director:
John Pylypczak, Diti Katona
Designer:
John Pylypczak

Client:
International Asset Management
Nature of Business:
Financial services
Design Firm:
Nesnadny & Schwartz
Art Director:
Okey Nestor, Mark Schwartz
Designer:
Okey Nestor

Client:
Southern Methodist University
Nature of Business:
University
Design Firm:
Sayles Graphic Design
Art Director:
John Sayles
Designer:
John Sayles

Client:
Oberoi Services
Nature of Business:
Spice Express Restaurant
Design Firm:
David Lancashire Design
Art Director:
Anne Aniulis
Designer:
David Lancashire
Photographer:
John Gollings

Client:
Electralure for Maxx Tech
Nature of Business:
Fishing tackle
Design Firm:
Three Communication Design
Art Director:
Three Communication Design
Designer:
Three Communication Design

Client:
Jay Vigon
Nature of Business:
T-shirts
Design Firm:
Jay Vigon Design & Art Direction
Art Director:
Jay Vigon
Designer:
Jay Vigon

Client:
Culinary Productions
Nature of Business:
Restaurant
Design Firm:
Louise Fili Ltd.
Art Director:
Louise Fili
Designer:
Louise Fili

Client:
Ministry of Schools of Slovenia
Nature of Business:
Voluntary Service Slovenia
Design Firm:
KROG
Art Director:
Edi Berk
Designer:
Edi Berk

Client:
Environment Canada
Nature of Business:
Environmental Protection Ministry
Design Firm:
Oasis Creative Group Inc.
Art Director:
Ted Larson
Designer:
Ted Larson

Client:
Ministry of Schools of Slovenia
Nature of Business:
Voluntary Service Slovenia
Design Firm:
KROG
Art Director:
Edi Berk
Designer:
Edi Berk

Client:
Wilshire Designs/Kata Division
Nature of Business:
Eyewear
Design Firm:
Studio Seireeni
Art Director:
Romane Cameron
Designer:
Romane Cameron

Fat Fish Films

Fat Fish Films

Fat Fish Films

Fat Fish Films 715 BAY VIEW DRIVE   MANHATTAN BEACH, CALIFORNIA 90266   TELEPHONE: 310 374 1843   FAX: 310 376 3054

Jacci Barrett

1A FLAXMAN COURT, WARDOUR STREET   LONDON W1V 3LB
TELEPHONE: 071 734 7186 · FAX: 071 734 0175

715 BAY VIEW DRIVE   MANHATTAN BEACH   CALIFORNIA 90266
TELEPHONE   310 374 1843   FAX   310 376 3054

715 BAY VIEW DRIVE
MANHATTAN BEACH, CALIFORNIA 90266
TELEPHONE: 310 374 1843
FAX: 310 376 3054

Client:
Complements
Nature of Business:
Gourmet fish sauce
Design Firm:
Bruce E. Morgan Graphic Design
Art Director:
Bruce E. Morgan
Designer:
Bruce E. Morgan

Client:
Colony Pictures
Nature of Business:
Motion pictures
Design Firm:
Donald E. Smolen & Associates
Art Director:
Donald E. Smolen
Designer:
J. Robert Faulkner

Client:
Z PrePress
Nature of Business:
Typography and prepress
Design Firm:
Arias Associates
Art Director:
Mauricio Arias
Designer:
Catherine Richards, Ellen Bruni
Illustrator:
Mauricio Arias

SOUP

French Onion, Soup of the Day: Cup 1.25   Bowl 1.95
Baked French Onion: 2.95

APPETIZERS

Fresh Baked Clams: Dozen 8.95   Half Dozen 5.95
Crab Filled Stuffed Mushrooms: 5.95   Barbecue Shrimp: 7.95
Roasted Red Peppers in Olive Oil: 4.95   Fried Calamari: 5.95
Baked Stuffed Artichoke with Lemon Garlic Butter: 3.95
Jumbo Shrimp Cocktail: 6.95   Garlic Bread: 2.50

SALADS

Eddie's Dressings: House, French, 1000 Island,
Creamy Garlic and Blue Cheese.
Eddie's House Salad: Romaine and Iceberg Lettuce, Artichoke Hearts,
Mushrooms, Tomatoes, Olives, Onions and Roasted Red Peppers 5.95
Pommadori: Beefsteak Tomatoes and Bermuda Onions
with Balsamic Vinaigrette. 4.25
Carpaccio: Seared Rare Beef Tenderloin, Spinach, Onions and
Mandarin Oranges with Hot Bacon Dressing 6.95
Caesar Salad: Creamy Garlic Dressing with Parmesan Cheese,
Croutons and Anchovies 4.75
Spinach and Shrimp Salad: Served with Tomato, Sliced Egg
and Balsamic Vinaigrette 4.25

VEGETABLES

Steamed Broccoli with Hollandaise Sauce: 2.95
Sauteed Mushrooms: 2.95   Broccoli and Mushrooms: 3.95
Spinach with Garlic and Oil: 2.95
Asparagus (In Season): Market Price

PASTA

Fettucini Alfredo: 9.95
Fettucine Alfredo with Primavera Vegetables: 11.95
Linguine with Red or White Clam Sauce: 9.95
Capellini, Linguine, Mostaccioli, Spaghetti or Fettuccine:
Choice of: Meat Sauce or Marinara 6.95
Italian Sausage or Meat Balls 7.95
Farfella Pasta: Bowtie Pasta with Sundried Tomatoes, Garlic,
Mushrooms and Olive Oil 9.95

EddieBull's

EST. 1992

RESTAURANT & BAR

When I was a kid, my two best friends in the whole world were
Eddie Bull and Scraps. Eddie was our English Bulldog. Scraps, a
mangy mutt who'd strayed into our hearts. Throughout my
young life, Eddie and Scraps were my constant companions. I swore
that in time, I'd do something to show my appreciation for all
their years of loyalty.
Well, every dog has his day. This is Eddie's. Sorry, Scraps.
I still owe you one. Maybe we'll name a dish after you someday.
Then again, maybe not.

January 2, 1992

Fresh Catch of the Day: Ask about our

All above entrees include soup and salad.
Also choice of potato, rice or pasta.

Client:
EddieBull's Restaurant & Bar
Nature of Business:
Restaurant and bar
Design Firm:
mpd/Michael Pagliuco Design
Art Director:
Michael Pagliuco
Designer:
Michael Pagliuco
Illustrator:
Paul Moch

Client:
Recticel International
Nature of Business:
Bedding products
Design Firm:
Design Board Behaeghel & Partners
Art Director:
Denis Keller
Designer:
Denis Keller

Client:
Puccinelli Design
Nature of Business:
Graphic design
Design Firm:
Puccinelli Design
Art Director:
Keith Puccinelli
Designer:
Keith Puccinelli
Assistant Designer:
Heidi Palladino

Client:
Ambattur Clothing Company
Nature of Business:
International wholesale clothing manufacturing
Design Firm:
Annette Harcus Design Pty. Ltd.
Art Director:
Annette Harcus
Designer:
Kristin Thieme, Annette Harcus

Client:
Ambattur Clothing Company
Nature of Business:
International wholesale clothing manufacturing
Design Firm:
Annette Harcus Design Pty. Ltd.
Art Director:
Annette Harcus
Designer:
Kristin Thieme, Annette Harcus

Client:
Unherd of Productions
Nature of Business:
Video production
Design Firm:
Ron Kellum Design
Art Director:
Ron Kellum
Designer:
Ron Kellum

Client:
Gang of Seven
Nature of Business:
Bicycle racing team
Design Firm:
Hornall Anderson Design Works
Art Director:
Jack Anderson
Designer:
Jack Anderson, Brian O'Neill

Client:
Berkner High School Rams
Nature of Business:
Class of '81 reunion
Design Firm:
Sibley/Peteet Design
Art Director:
John Evans
Designer:
John Evans

Client:
Gang of Seven
Nature of Business:
Bicycle racing team
Design Firm:
Hornall Anderson Design Works
Art Director:
Jack Anderson
Designer:
Jack Anderson, Brian O'Neill

Client:
Integrus
Nature of Business:
Architecture
Design Firm:
Hornall Anderson Design Works
Art Director:
John Hornall
Designer:
John Hornall, Paula Cox, Brian O'Neill,
Lian Ng

RAMSTONE

A Division of   2504 Camino Entrada

Advanced   Santa Fe, NM 87505

Design   505-473-9419

Technologies   800-635-7551

                   FAX-505-473-5519

RAMSTONE

Emily Garcia   2504 Camino Entrada

Sales Manager   Santa Fe, NM 87505

                   505-473-9419

                   800-635-7551

                   FAX-505-473-5519

RAMSTONE

2504 Camino Entrada

Santa Fe, NM 87505

Client:

Blenz Coffee Franchise

Nature of Business:

Coffee and capuccino Bar

Design Firm:

Siren Design Studios

Art Director:

Jim Yue

Designer:

Jim Yue

Illustrator:

David Cheng

Client:

Brio Espresso Bar

Nature of Business:

Gourmet coffee and snack bar

Design Firm:

Mark Mock Design Associates, Inc.

Art Director:

Mark Mock

Designer:

Jennifer Gilliland

Client:

Java Joe's

Nature of Business:

Coffeehouse

Design Firm:

Sayles Graphic Design

Art Director:

John Sayles

Designer:

John Sayles

Texas Biotechnology
Corporation

7000 Fannin
Houston TX 77030
Telephone 713-796-8822
Fax 713-796-9330

Texas Biotechnology
Corporation

7000 Fannin
Houston TX 77030

Client:
Texas Biotechnology
Nature of Business:
Biotech research
Design Firm:
Pentagram Design
Art Director:
Michael Gericke
Designer:
Michael Gericke, Donna Ching

Client:
MGL
Nature of Business:
Town Theatre of Ljubljana
Design Firm:
KROG
Art Director:
Edi Berk
Designer:
Edi Berk

Client:
Made in Taiwan
Nature of Business:
Symbol of excellence for Taiwan-made products
Design Firm:
Bright & Associates
Art Director:
Keith Bright
Designer:
Raymond Wood

Client:
Canadian Pacific Forest Products Limited
Nature of Business:
Forest products
Design Firm:
Gottschalk+Ash International
Art Director:
Stuart Ash
Designer:
Stuart Ash

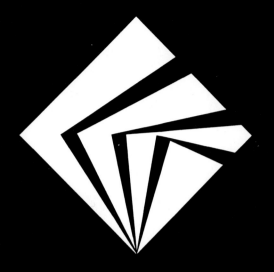

Client:
Marketing International Corporation
Nature of Business:
Trade show management
Design Firm:
MacVicar Design & Communications
Art Director:
John Vance
Designer:
William A. Gordon

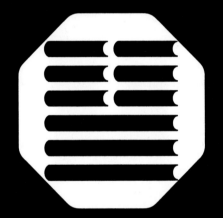

Client:
Juxian Guan Ltd.
Nature of Business:
Publishing
Design Firm:
Kan Tai-keung Design & Associates Ltd.
Art Director:
Kan Tai-keung
Designer:
Kan Tai-keung
Creative Director:
Kan Tai-keung

Client:
Western Digital Corporation
Nature of Business:
Computers
Design Firm:
Bright & Associates
Art Director:
Keith Bright
Designer:
Raymond Wood

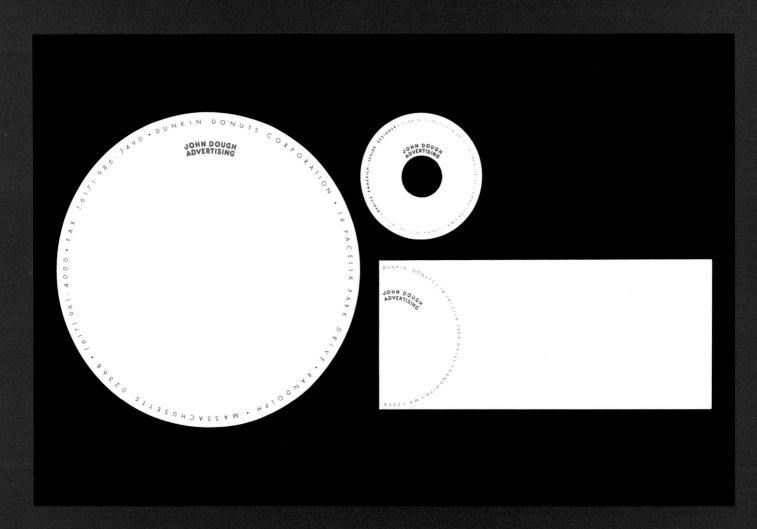

Client:
John Dough Advertising
Nature of Business:
Advertising agency for Dunkin' Donuts
Design Firm:
John Dough Advertising
Art Director:
Denise Emmerich
Designer:
Denise Emmerich

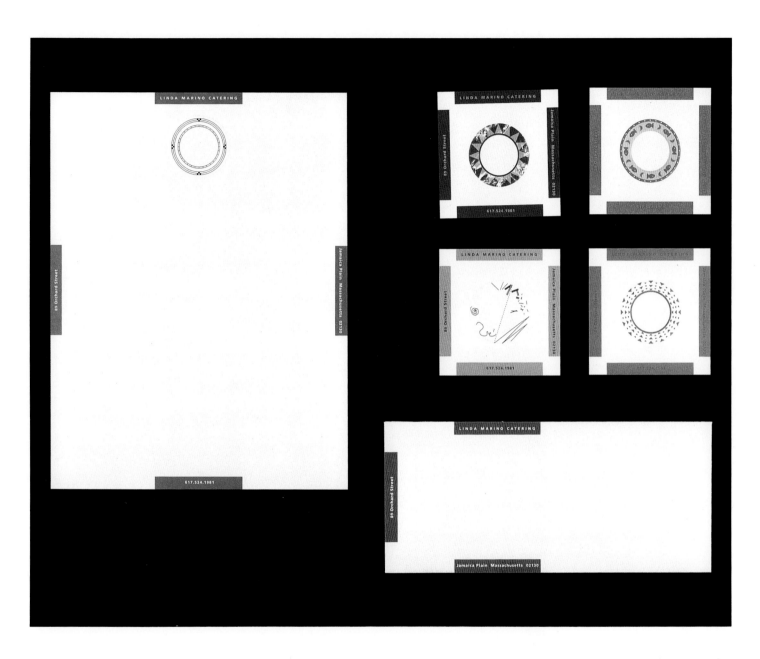

Client:
Linda Marino Catering
Nature of Business:
Catering
Design Firm:
plus design inc.
Art Director:
Anita Meyer
Designer:
Anita Meyer
Printer:
Aldus Press
Embosser:
McEmbossing

Client:
The Light Car Company Limited
Nature of Business:
Car manufacturing and designing
Design Firm:
The Team
Art Director:
Richard Ward
Designer:
Richard Ward

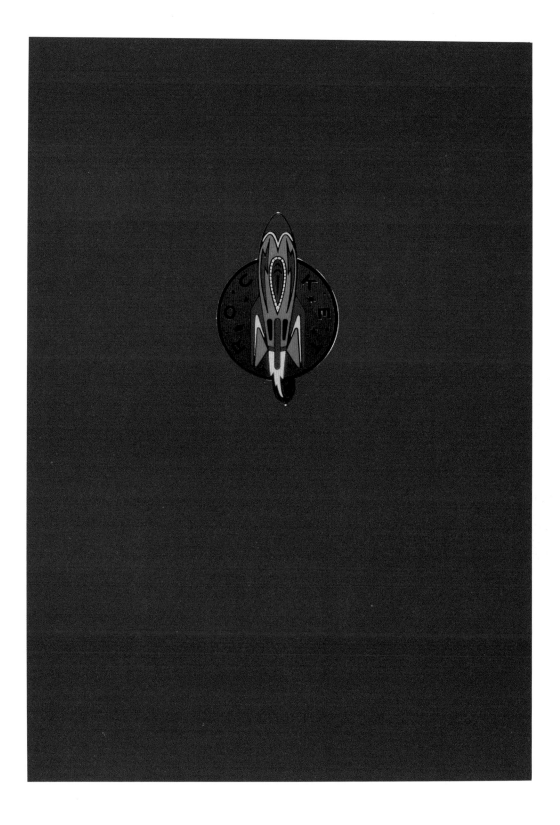

Client:
Sayles Graphic Design
Nature of Business:
Graphic design
Design Firm:
Sayles Graphic Design
Art Director:
John Sayles
Designer:
John Sayles

Client:
Trata
Nature of Business:
Upscale seafood restaurant
Design Firm:
Graphème Communication-Design
Art Director:
Michael Dempsey
Designer:
Susan Mosdell

Client:
Pacific Guest Suites
Nature of Business:
Extended-stay accommodations
Design Firm:
Hornall Anderson Design Works
Art Director:
Julia LaPine
Designer:
Julia LaPine

Client:
Pacific Guest Suites
Nature of Business:
Extended-stay accommodations
Design Firm:
Hornall Anderson Design Works
Art Director:
Julia LaPine
Designer:
Julia LaPine

Client:
Fleuriste des Tours
Nature of Business:
Florist
Design Firm:
Graphème Communication-Design
Art Director:
Pierre Léonard
Designer:
Pierre Léonard

FLEURISTE
DES
TOURS

Client:
Le Supre Diamant de Coulture de Make
Nature of Business:
Diamond jewelry
Design Firm:
Douglas Design Office
Art Director:
Douglas Doolittle
Designer:
Douglas Doolittle

Client:
Le Supre Diamant de Coulture de Make
Nature of Business:
Diamond jewelry
Design Firm:
Douglas Design Office
Art Director:
Douglas Doolittle
Designer:
Douglas Doolittle

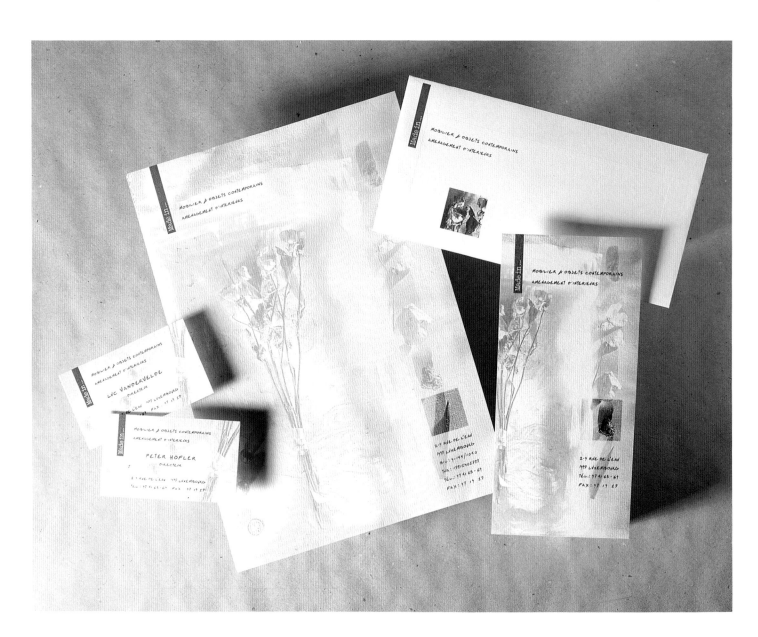

Client:
Made In
Nature of Business:
Interior design
Design Firm:
Made by Sams
Art Director:
Sunthia Seng-Kreutz
Designer:
Christine Feck

paRDiseño

campos

eliseos 200-6

col. polanco,

mexico, d.f.

tel 254 27 53

fax 203 42 85

campos

eliseos 200-6

col. polanco,

mexico, d.f.

tel 254 27 53

fax 203 42 85

paRDiseño

d.g.alvaro legía a.

paRDiseño

campos

eliseos 200-6

polanco,

mexico, d.f.

254 27 53

203 42 85

Client:
Hartford Restaurant Association
Nature of Business:
Restaurant association
Design Firm:
Dennis Russo Design
Art Director:
Dennis Russo
Designer:
Maria F. Mota

Client:
Italia
Nature of Business:
Italian restaurant
Design Firm:
Hornall Anderson Design Works
Art Director:
Jack Anderson
Designer:
Jack Anderson, Julia LaPine

Client:
Santa Barbara Bread Company
Nature of Business:
Breadmaker
Design Firm:
Rusty Kay & Associates
Art Director:
Rusty Kay
Designer:
Susan Rogers

Client:
Suzanne Ainslie
Nature of Business:
Healthy dining guide
Design Firm:
Schowalter2 Design
Art Director:
Toni Schowalter
Designer:
Ilene Price

Client:
National Travelers Life
Nature of Business:
Insurance

Client:
Northern Telecom Limited
Nature of Business:
Telecommunications
Design Firm:
Concrete Design Communications Inc.
Art Director:
John Pylypczak, Diti Katona
Designer:
John Pylypczak

Client:
Rama Villas
Nature of Business:
Resort
Design Firm:
Schowalter2 Design
Art Director:
Toni Schowalter
Designer:
Ilene Price

Client:
Travel Services of America
Nature of Business:
Travel agency
Design Firm:
Hornall Anderson Design Works
Art Director:
Jack Anderson
Designer:
Jack Anderson, David Bates,
Julia LaPine, Mary Hermes

Client:
Nike Design
Nature of Business:
Sports and fitness apparel and shoes
Design Firm:
Nike Design
Art Director:
Ron Dumas
Designer:
Ross Patrick
Illustrator:
Ross Patrick

Client:
Pinball Clothing
Nature of Business:
Men's casualwear
Design Firm:
Annette Harcus Design Pty. Ltd.
Art Director:
Annette Harcus
Designer:
Kristin Thieme, Annette Harcus

Client:
BrooksHoward
Nature of Business:
CD and video duplication
Design Firm:
Evenson Design Group
Art Director:
Stan Evenson
Designer:
Stan Evenson, Glenn Sakamoto

152

Client:
Southeastern Conference
Nature of Business:
Regional collegiate athletic association
Design Firm:
FitzMartin Design Partners
Art Director:
Sean Doyle
Designer:
Randy Sims

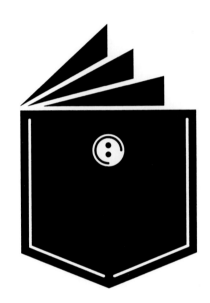

Client:
Asymetrix Corporation
Nature of Business:
Software products
Design Firm:
Hornall Anderson Design Works
Art Director:
Jack Anderson
Designer:
Jack Anderson, Julie Tanagi-Lock,
Mary Hermes, Lian Ng

Client:
Broadway Agencies Ltd.
Nature of Business:
Insurance agents and brokers
Design Firm:
Siren Design Studios
Art Director:
Hamazaki & Wong Advertising
Designer:
David Cheng

Client:
Japan Singapore AI Centre
Nature of Business:
First Singapore international conference
on intelligent systems
Design Firm:
Design Objectives Pte. Ltd.
Art Director:
Ronnie S.C. Tan
Designer:
Ronnie Tan, Ong Lin

Client:
Hammersly Technology Partners, Inc.
Nature of Business:
Computer software
Design Firm:
IDEAS
Art Director:
Robin Brandes
Designer:
Robin Brandes

Client:
Komunalna operativa
Nature of Business:
Communal works
Design Firm:
KROG
Art Director:
Edi Berk
Designer:
Edi Berk

Client:
Richard Reens
Nature of Business:
Photographer
Design Firm:
RBMM
Art Director:
Luis D. Acevedo
Designer:
Luis D. Acevedo

Client:
Canadian Museum of Nature
Nature of Business:
Museum
Design Firm:
Gottschalk+Ash International
Art Director:
Peter Steiner
Designer:
Michael Wou

Canadian
Museum
of Nature

Musée
canadien
de la nature

Canadian
Museum
of Nature

Musée
canadien
de la nature

Louise Damant
Executive Assistant
to the Deputy Director

P.O. Box 3443, Station "D"
Ottawa, Ontario
Canada K1P 6P4

Tel. (613) 992-9370
Fax (613) 995-3040

Canadian
Museum
of Nature

Musée
canadien
de la nature

P.O. Box 3443, Station "D" | C.P. 3443, Succursale "D"
Ottawa, Canada | Ottawa, Canada
K1P 6P4 | K1P 6P4

Client:
Canadian Museum of Nature
Nature of Business:
Museum
Design Firm:
Gottschalk+Ash International
Art Director:
Peter Steiner
Designer:
Michael Wou

Client:
U S West NewVector Group
Nature of Business:
Quest for Quality/Communications
Design Firm:
Hornall Anderson Design Works
Art Director:
Jack Anderson
Designer:
Jack Anderson, Jani Drewfs,
David Bates

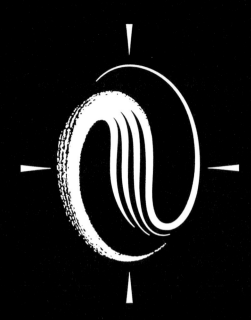

Client:
Urban Communications
Nature of Business:
Planning company
Design Firm:
Douglas Design Office
Art Director:
Douglas Doolittle
Designer:
Douglas Doolittle

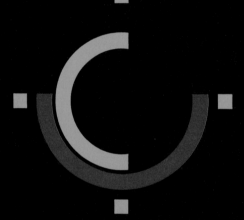

Client:
Ikko Ohchi, México
Nature of Business:
Traditional Japanese music
Design Firm:
Félix Beltrán & Asociados
Art Director:
Félix Beltrán
Designer:
Félix Beltrán

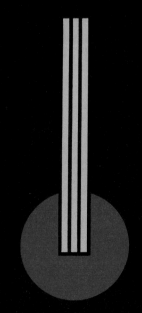

Client:
Urban Communications
Nature of Business:
Planning company
Design Firm:
Douglas Design Office
Art Director:
Douglas Doolittle
Designer:
Douglas Doolittle

159

Client:
Tian An China Investments Co. Ltd.
Nature of Business:
Investment group
Design Firm:
Kan Tai-keung Design & Associates Ltd.
Art Director:
Kan Tai-keung, Freeman Lau Siu Hong
Designer:
Freeman Lau Siu Hong
Creative Director:
Kan Tai-keung

Client:
Totem Co. Ltd.
Nature of Business:
Art and product design
Design Firm:
Douglas Design Office
Art Director:
Douglas Doolittle
Designer:
Douglas Doolittle

Client:
Ontario Government of Canada
Nature of Business:
Design exposition
Design Firm:
Douglas Design Office
Art Director:
Douglas Doolittle
Designer:
Douglas Doolittle
Illustrator:
Mr. Yoshida

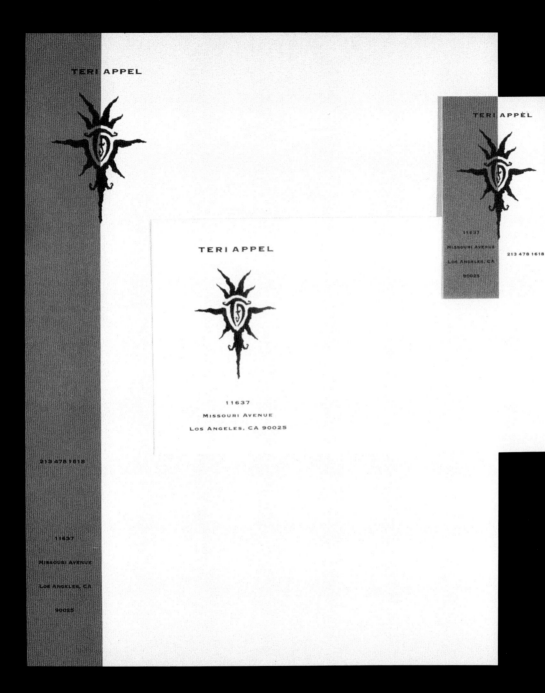

Client:
Teri Appel
Nature of Business:
Editor and writer on design, style,
and architecture
Design Firm:
Richard Wilks Design
Art Director:
Richard Wilks
Designer:
Richard Wilks

Client:
City of Ballarat
Nature of Business:
Performing Arts Centre
Design Firm:
Pen and Paper
Art Director:
Peter Lambert
Designer:
Peter Lambert, Richard Jeziorny

Client:
P.S.P. (PolyGram Special Products)
Nature of Business:
Record company
Design Firm:
PolyGram records
Art Director:
Chris Thompson
Designer:
Giulio Turturro
Creative Director:
Michael Bays

Client:
Jim and Diane Bremer
Nature of Business:
Wedding
Design Firm:
Sibley/Peteet Design
Art Director:
Jim Bremer, Diane Bremer
Designer:
David Lloyd Beck
Illustrator:
David Lloyd Beck
Copywriter:
Kevin Orlin Johnson

162

Client:
Jim and Diane Bremer
Nature of Business:
Wedding
Design Firm:
Sibley/Peteet Design
Art Director:
Jim Bremer, Diane Bremer
Designer:
David Lloyd Beck
Illustrator:
David Lloyd Beck

Client:
Marat Viktor Beljajev
Nature of Business:
Graphic design
Design Firm:
Vácant Designer
Art Director:
Marat Viktor Beljajev
Designer:
Marat Viktor Beljajev

Client:
Aspen Design Conference
Nature of Business:
Convention
Design Firm:
Steven Guarnaccia
Art Director:
Steven Guarnaccia
Designer:
Steven Guarnaccia

Client:
American Academy of Achievement
Nature of Business:
Museum
Design Firm:
Pentagram Design, Inc.
Art Director:
Kit Hinrichs
Designer:
Jackie Foshaug

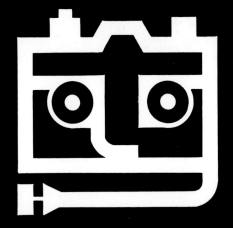

Client:
Stan Barouh
Nature of Business:
Photography
Design Firm:
Market Sights, Inc.
Art Director:
Marilyn Worseldine
Designer:
Marilyn Worseldine

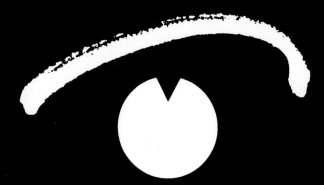

Client:
Children's Institute for Eye Research
Nature of Business:
Eyecare
Design Firm:
Bright & Associates
Art Director:
Keith Bright
Designer:
Mark Verlander

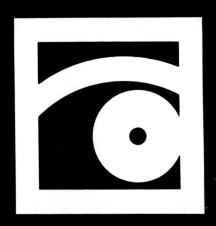

Client:
Decision Strategies International
Nature of Business:
Management Consultants
Design Firm:
Schowalter2 Design
Art Director:
Toni Schowalter
Designer:
Toni Schowalter

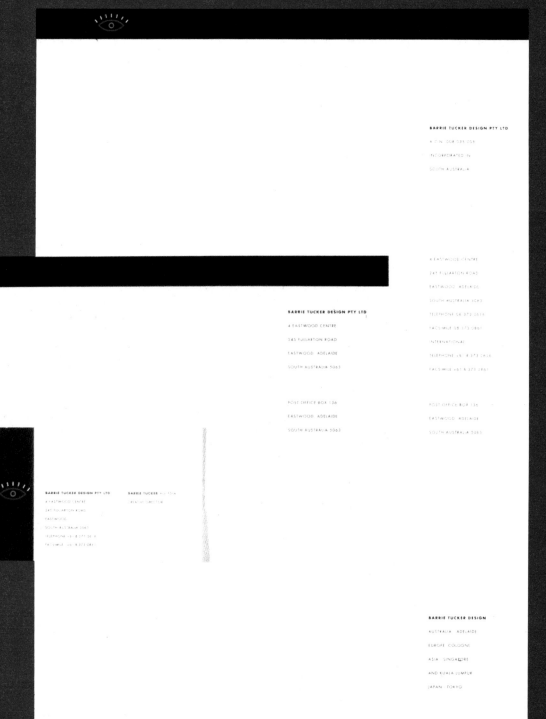

Client:
Barrie Tucker Design Pty. Ltd.
Nature of Business:
Design consulting
Design Firm:
Barrie Tucker Design Pty. Ltd.
Art Director:
Barrie Tucker
Designer:
Barrie Tucker
Finished Art:
Jody Tucker, Claire Rose

Client:
Barrie Tucker Design Pty. Ltd.
Nature of Business:
Design consulting
Design Firm:
Barrie Tucker Design Pty. Ltd.
Art Director:
Barrie Tucker
Designer:
Barrie Tucker
Finished Art:
Jody Tucker, Claire Rose

Client:
Palm Springs International Film Festival
Nature of Business:
Annual event
Design Firm:
Mark Palmer Design
Art Director:
Mark Palmer
Designer:
Mark Palmer
Computer Production:
Curtis Palmer

Client:
Great Date
Nature of Business:
Date growing and distribution
Design Firm:
Mark Palmer Design
Art Director:
Mark Palmer
Designer:
Mark Palmer
Computer Production:
Curtis Palmer

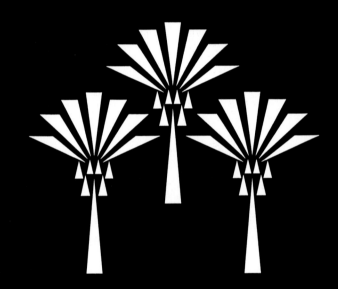

Client:
Friend Hebrew University
Nature of Business:
Tree Fund
Design Firm:
One Ahead Graphic Design Studio Pty. Ltd.
Art Director:
Raphael Klaesi
Designer:
Raphael Klaesi

Client:
Bell Mountain Winery
Nature of Business:
Winemaker
Design Firm:
RBMM
Art Director:
Horacio Cobos, Luis Acevedo
Designer:
Horacio Cobos

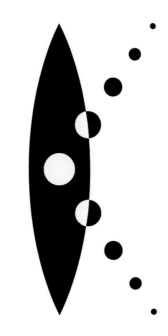

Client:
Steve Keough Photography Pty. Ltd.
Nature of Business:
Photography
Design Firm:
Barrie Tucker Design Pty. Ltd.
Art Director:
Barrie Tucker
Designer:
Barrie Tucker
Computer Graphics:
Jody Tucker

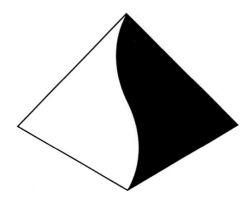

Client:
Soft Solutions
Nature of Business:
Informational software development
Design Firm:
Alancheril Design
Art Director:
Mat Alancheril
Designer:
Mat Alancheril

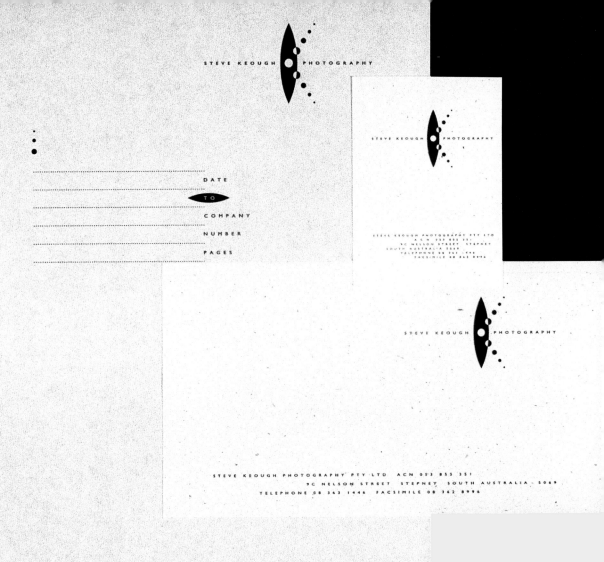

STEVE KEOUGH PHOTOGRAPHY

STEVE KEOUGH PHOTOGRAPHY

DATE

TO

COMPANY

NUMBER

PAGES

STEVE KEOUGH PHOTOGRAPHY PTY LTD
A.C.N. 053 855 351
9C NELSON STREET STEPNEY
SOUTH AUSTRALIA 5069
TELEPHONE 08 363 1446
FACSIMILE 08 362 8996

STEVE KEOUGH PHOTOGRAPHY

STEVE KEOUGH PHOTOGRAPHY PTY LTD   ACN 053 855 351
9C NELSON STREET   STEPNEY   SOUTH AUSTRALIA - 5069
TELEPHONE 08 363 1446   FACSIMILE 08 362 8996

STEVE KEOUGH PHOTOGRAPHY PTY LTD   A.C.N. 053 855 351
9C NELSON STREET   STEPNEY   SOUTH AUSTRALIA   5069
TELEPHONE 08 363 1446   FACSIMILE 08 362 8996

Client:
Steve Keough Photography Pty. Ltd.
Nature of Business:
Photography
Design Firm:
Barrie Tucker Design Pty. Ltd.
Art Director:
Barrie Tucker
Designer:
Barrie Tucker
Computer Graphics:
Jody Tucker

Client:
Country Select Potato Chips
Nature of Business:
Kettle-style chips made from
organically grown potatoes
Design Firm:
Siren Design Studios
Art Director:
Jim Yue
Designer:
David Cheng

Client:
National Museum of Science and Technology
Nature of Business:
Amazing Potato exhibition
Design Firm:
Concrete Design Communications, Inc.
Art Director:
John Pylypczak, Diti Katona
Designer:
John Pylypczak

Client:
St. Rita School for the Deaf
Nature of Business:
Grade through high school for deaf children
Design Firm:
Design Team One, Inc.
Art Director:
Dan Bittman
Designer:
Dan Bittman

Client:
Todd Ware Massage
Nature of Business:
Massage
Design Firm:
The Weller Institute for the Cure of Design, Inc.
Art Director:
Don Weller
Designer:
Don Weller

TODD WARE

MASSAGE

649-1568

TODD WARE

ATHLETIC MASSAGE
SKIN & CELLULITE TREATMENTS
SWEDISH MASSAGE
JIN SHIN DO / ACCUPRESSURE
MUSCULAR REEDUCATION
EGENESIS / BIOENERGETICS

HOME
649-1568

PHONE MAIL
1-468-6273

Client:
Mirror Mountain Motorcycles
Nature of Business:
Motorbike restoration
Design Firm:
Planet Design Co.
Art Director:
Kevin Wade, Dana Lytle
Designer:
Tom Jenkins

Client:
AG Communication Systems
Nature of Business:
Promo logo
Design Firm:
AG Communication Systems Design Group
Art Director:
Jeffrey Moss
Designer:
Jeffrey Moss

Client:
Richard Reens
Nature of Business:
Photographer
Design Firm:
RBMM
Art Director:
Luis D. Acevedo
Designer:
Luis D. Acevedo

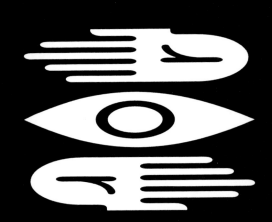

Client:
Our Savior's Community, A Lutheran Church
Nature of Business:
Lutheran church
Design Firm:
Mark Palmer Design
Art Director:
Mark Palmer
Designer:
Mark Palmer
Computer Production:
Curtis Palmer

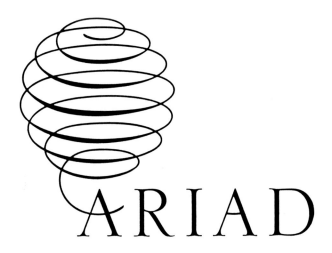

Client:
Ariad
Nature of Business:
Biotechnology research
Design Firm:
Pentagram Design
Art Director:
Woody Pirtle
Designer:
Susan Hochbaum

Client:
Alan Chan Creations Ltd.
Nature of Business:
Trading Company
Design Firm:
Alan Chan Design Company
Art Director:
Alan Chan
Designer:
Alan Chan

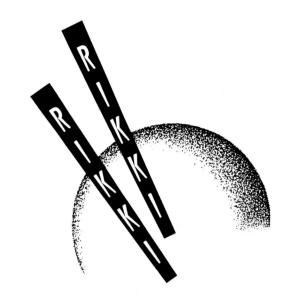

Client:
Rikki Rikki
Nature of Business:
Japanese restaurant
Design Firm:
Hornall Anderson Design Works
Art Director:
Jack Anderson
Designer:
Jack Anderson, David Bates, Lian Ng

Client:
Lend Lease
Nature of Business:
Youth retail precinct within shopping center
Design Firm:
Annette Harcus Design Pty. Ltd.
Art Director:
Annette Harcus
Designer:
Kristin Thieme, Annette Harcus

Client:
M.H. Podell Co.
Nature of Business:
Construction
Design Firm:
Sam Smidt Inc.
Art Director:
Sam Smidt
Designer:
Sam Smidt

Client:
BKK Lite 97 FM
Nature of Business:
Radio station
Design Firm:
Supon Design Group
Art Director:
Supon Phornirunlit
Designer:
Andrew Dolan

Client:
Texas Association of
Landscape Professionals
Nature of Business:
Christmas social/
Landscape association
Design Firm:
Sibley/Peteet Design
Art Director:
John Evans
Designer:
John Evans

Client:
Thomas Hayward Auctioneers
Nature of Business:
Auctioneering
Design Firm:
Pentagram Design, Inc.
Art Director:
Lowell Williams
Designer:
Bill Carson

Client:
BKK Lite 97 FM
Nature of Business:
Radio station
Design Firm:
Supon Design Group
Art Director:
Supon Phornirunlit
Designer:
Andrew Dolan

Qualipige

40, AVENUE DE SEGUR 75015 PARIS
TEL: 45.67.00.08 • FAX: 45.67.00.85

Qualipige

TEL: 45.67.00.08
FAX: 45.00.85
•
40 AVENUE DE SEGUR
75015 PARIS

Client:
Qualipige
Nature of Business:
Advertising
Design Firm:
Design Cornu-Malcourant
Art Director:
Véronique Malcourant, Jean Michel Cornu
Designer:
Véronique Malcourant, Jean Michel Cornu

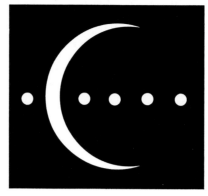

Client:
Celestial Harmonies
Nature of Business:
Music production
Design Firm:
Boelts Bros. Design
Art Director:
Jackson Boelts, Eric Boelts
Designer:
Jackson Boelts, Eric Boelts,
Kerry Stratford, Eckart Rahn

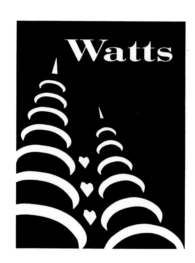

Client:
CDAC
Nature of Business:
Community Development Advisory Committee
Design Firm:
CRA.LA
Art Director:
Terence Mitchell
Designer:
Ann Greenwood

Client:
Grafikhaus Inc., Film & Video Division
Nature of Business:
Design
Design Firm:
AG Communication Systems Design Group
Art Director:
Jeffrey Moss
Designer:
Jeffrey Moss

FAHRENHEIT N.Y.

101 5TH AVENUE, 3RD FL

NEW YORK, NY 10003

TEL. (212) 807-9440

FAX (212) 807-9503

FAHRENHEIT CHI

211 EAST OHIO

CHICAGO, IL 60611

TEL. (312) 787-8811

FAX (312) 661-0071

FAHRENHEIT L.A.

1419 SECOND STREET

SANTA MONICA, CA 90401

TEL. (310) 319-1991

FAX (310) 394-2903

DAVIS

DAVIS

FAHRENHEIT N.Y.
101 5TH AVENUE, 3RD FL
NEW YORK, NY 10003
TEL. (212) 807-9440
FAX (212) 807-9503

FAHRENHEIT CHI
211 EAST OHIO
CHICAGO, IL 60611
TEL. (312) 787-8811
FAX (312) 661-0071

FAHRENHEIT L.A.
1419 SECOND STREET
SANTA MONICA, CA 90401
TEL. (310) 319-1991
FAX (310) 394-2903

Client:
Fahrenheit Films
Nature of Business:
Film production
Design Firm:
Jay Vigon Design & Art Direction
Art Director:
Jay Vigon
Designer:
Jay Vigon

Client:
San Francisco International Film Festival
Nature of Business:
Poster advertising event
Design Firm:
Landor Associates
Art Director:
Terry Irwin, Rachel Wear
Production Artist:
Peter Kesselman

INTERNATIONAL CORPORATE VIDEO, INC.

1020 Serpentine Lane
Suite 114
Pleasanton, CA 94566
(415)426-8230
Fax: (415)426-8330

INTERNATIONAL CORPORATE VIDEO, INC.

1020 Serpentine Lane
Suite 114
Pleasanton, CA 94566

David Dunham
Production
1020 Serpentine Lane
Suite 114
Pleasanton, CA 94566
(510)426-8230
Fax: (510)426-8330

INTERNATIONAL CORPORATE VIDEO, INC.

Client:
International Corporate Video
Nature of Business:
Video production
Design Firm:
Shawver Associates
Art Director:
Mark Shawver
Designer:
Brian Kuehn

Client:
Stan Barouh
Nature of Business:
Photography
Design Firm:
Market Sights, Inc.
Art Director:
Marilyn Worseldine
Designer:
Marilyn Worseldine

Client:
Chicago Heart Association
Nature of Business:
Annual benefit
Design Firm:
JOED Design Inc.
Art Director:
Edward Rebek
Designer:
Edward Rebek

Client:
Photo Resource Pty. Ltd.
Nature of Business:
Photography supplies retailing
Design Firm:
Mammoliti Chan Design
Art Director:
Tony Mammoliti
Designer:
Tony Mammoliti, Chwee Kuan Chan

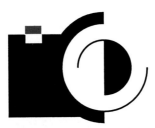

Photo Resource

Industrial
Photographic
Supplies

Peter D'Abbs
Director

Photo Resource Pty Ltd

Industrial
Photographic Supplies
117 Queens Pde/Box 344
Clifton Hill, Vic. 3068
Tel 03 481 5200
Fax 03 482 3374

Photo Resource Pty Ltd
117 Queens Parade
P.O. Box 344
Clifton Hill
Victoria 3068
Tel 03 481 5200
Fax 03 482 3374

Client:
Photo Resource Pty. Ltd.
Nature of Business:

Client:
Brookstone
Nature of Business:
Specialty tool and gift retailing
Design Firm:
Pentagram Design
Art Director:
Michael Bierut
Designer:
Michael Bierut, Dorit Lev

INDICES

INDEX BY CLIENT

INDEX BY CLIENT

INDEX BY DESIGN FIRM

INDEX BY DESIGN FIRM

INDEX BY ART DIRECTOR & DESIGNER

INDEX BY ART DIRECTOR & DESIGNER